The Philosophy
of Protest

The Philosophy of Protest

Fighting for Justice Without Going to War

Jennifer Kling and Megan Mitchell

ROWMAN & LITTLEFIELD
Lanham • Boulder • New York • London

Published by Rowman & Littlefield
An imprint of The Rowman & Littlefield Publishing Group, Inc.
4501 Forbes Boulevard, Suite 200, Lanham, Maryland 20706
www.rowman.com

86-90 Paul Street, London EC2A 4NE

British Library Cataloguing in Publication Information Available

Library of Congress Cataloging-in-Publication Data

Names: Kling, Jennifer, 1984- author. | Mitchell, Megan, 1983- author.
Title: The philosophy of protest : fighting for justice without going to war / Jennifer Kling and Megan Mitchell.
Description: Lanham, Maryland : Rowman & Littlefield, [2022] | Includes bibliographical references and index. | Summary: "Examines how protest is practiced and argues that suitably constrained violent political protest is sometimes justified"— Provided by publisher.
Identifiers: LCCN 2021035444 (print) | LCCN 2021035445 (ebook) | ISBN 9781786613202 (hardcover) | ISBN 9781538188149 (paper) | ISBN 9781786613219 (epub)
Subjects: LCSH: Social movements—Philosophy. | Political violence. | Violence.
Classification: LCC HM883 .K55 2022 (print) | LCC HM883 (ebook) | DDC 303.48/4—dc3
LC record available at https://lccn.loc.gov/2021035444
LC ebook record available at https://lccn.loc.gov/2021035445

Contents

Acknowledgments

The basic idea for this book was born during long late-night walks as we studied together for our comprehensive exams in graduate school. However, it never would have materialized if not for the many people who encouraged us to think through these ideas and write them down along the way. Thank you, friends, colleagues, and advisors! A special thanks to the editors at Radical Philosophy Review and audiences at Concerned Philosophers for Peace, the Virginia Tech Philosophy Department, the Association for Practical and Professional Ethics, and the International Society for Military Ethics.

We would also like to thank our shared dissertation advisor, Dr. Bernard Boxill. Bernie never took up the so-called philosophical view from nowhere; his deep challenges to us, throughout graduate school and beyond, come from thinking through what it's like to live in a complicated, imperfect, messy, rich, and beautiful world. If this book reflects even some of Bernie's philosophical prowess, we are proud of it.

This book was written at Stonehill College and at the University of Colorado, Colorado Springs. Colleges and universities, for all their foibles, make the world a brighter place. Our thanks to the communities at both schools.

Finally, our deepest appreciation to our respective partners, Patrick and Kevin, who kept us fed and somewhat sane during this process. This book is dedicated to Kaylee, whose Zoom bombs, dragon masks, and general 7-year-old-ness made writing a book during a global pandemic possible and sometimes even fun. May she grow up to live in a world where protest is no longer needed.

Preface

On October 5, 2000, heavy equipment operator Ljubisav Đokić fired up his wheel loader and charged at the Radio Television of Serbia (RTS) building in Belgrade, Serbia. RTS was widely seen as the mouthpiece of Slobodan Milošević's rule. Đokić's actions were part of widespread protests in Belgrade and around the country in response to the falsification of the September 2000 election results and Milošević's refusal to concede power. Later that day, Serbian civilians overran the parliament building and, upon their discovery of several thousand ballots pre-marked for Milošević, partially burned it down. Serbian security forces refused to crack down on the protesters, and on October 7, 2000, Milošević resigned.[1]

This day-long series of events is sometimes called the "Bulldozer Protests" or the "Bulldozer Revolution" after Đokić's memorable actions. Touted as a victory for democracy by several Western media outlets, the Bulldozer Protests/Revolution invite us to consider how we should think about protest, violence, and revolution. Was burning the parliament an act of protest? What about charging a building with a bulldozer? Or are these properly understood as instances of riotous violence? Should they perhaps be considered insurrectionary or revolutionary acts?

Certainly, the inclination has been to refer to these incidents as protests, and to the change of power as a whole (from Milošević to Vojislav Koštunica), as either a successful protest or a nonviolent revolution. Although sixty-five people were injured, and two died during the

October 5 events—one from a heart attack and one from an accidental, yet fatal, fall in front of a moving front loader—the general consensus is that the Serbian Bulldozer Protests/Revolution was one of the most successful nonviolent political actions in recent history. It is often celebrated as a paradigm case of the power of nonviolent protest and is pointed to as an exemplar that other pro-democracy groups around the world should emulate.[2]

Contrast this with a more recent case, which occurred on January 6, 2021, in Washington, D.C. There, thousands of people, who believed that the 2020 U.S. Presidential election had been stolen, overran the U.S. Capitol building in an attempt to stop the Congressional certification of the electoral votes. In the process, about 140 people were injured and 5 people died—1 police officer was killed by rioters, 1 rioter was shot by Capitol police, 1 rioter was crushed to death by other rioters, and 2 rioters died from a heart attack and stroke, respectively.[3] While the groups did not use fire in this case, there was property damage similar to what occurred in Serbia throughout the U.S. Capitol and surrounding federal buildings.[4]

Although these Americans, much like the Serbian protesters, believed they were acting to protect and further democracy, the public response was markedly different. Mainstream media widely condemned the attacks. Outside of far-right circles, they were not trumpeted as an attempted defense of democracy, or even as a kind of well-meaning, although misguided, protest or revolution. As newly certified U.S. President Joe Biden said, in response to the attacks, "Don't dare call them protesters. They were a riotous mob. Insurrectionists. Domestic terrorists. It's that basic. It's that simple."[5]

There are differences between the two cases. Most importantly, the Serbians' belief that the democratic process in their country was being undermined was true, and the Americans' similar belief in 2021 was false. The cases do share key structural similarities though, that raise important questions about the nature of protest, violence, and revolution. Intuitively, we want to praise and laud the 2000 Bulldozer Protests/Revolution, and draw attention to it as an instance of protest. At the same time, we want to criticize and condemn the 2021 Capitol Riot/Insurrection, and draw attention to it as an instance of rioting and (perhaps) insurrection. However, if we take up the common contemporary liberal understanding of protest, it is difficult to see how we can support these intuitions by drawing a principled distinction between the two cases.

Liberal societies are supposed to, among other things, respect reasonable disagreement between their members.[6] In line with that commitment, we might think we should be neutral here, and so say that however we end up categorizing these two cases, their categorizations must go together. Either both are cases of protest, or both are cases of violent insurrection, or both are cases of riotous mobs engaging in domestic terrorism, or both are cases of attempted/actual revolution. As Kimberley Brownlee argues, for something to count as civil disobedience or lawbreaking protest, it must be a public, "conscientious communicative breach of law motivated by steadfast, sincere, and serious, though possibly mistaken, moral commitment."[7] Crucially, for some political action to count as protest, on the liberal conception, it need not be *right*; that is, it need not be in the service of justice.[8] It must only meet the three process constraints of being public, conscientious, and communicative. If both the Serbian Bulldozer Protests/Revolution and the U.S. Capitol Riot/Insurrection meet those criteria, then they both count as protest (justified or not).

We might think this is all beside the point, however—the first question to ask is whether they were violent. In contemporary liberal societies, this is the issue on which all else seems to turn. It is widely believed, almost as an article of faith, that political actions must be *nonviolent* to count as protest. If complete nonviolence is a necessary constraint, then both cases fail to be instances of protest. What they are is still open to question; however, we could say, and many people do in fact say, that we know what they are not. The Serbians and Americans were violent—therefore, whatever they were, and whatever the justice or injustice of their causes, they were not protesters.

We reject this conclusion. In contemporary liberal societies marked by severe and ongoing oppression, it is not true that all protest—to count as protest—must be wholly nonviolent. We argue that sometimes, nonlethal violence is a legitimate and effective way to politically communicate about the injustices that are present in a liberal society. It is not violence that disqualifies the Serbians and Americans as protesters. Rather, whether they are protesters depends on whether their violence was legitimate, effective, and politically communicative about actual injustices in their societies.

In chapter 1, we argue that the current liberal conception of protest is insufficient and inappropriate for the contemporary political landscape. We find ourselves in a world where people live under conditions of serious oppression in ostensibly liberal societies. According to the international laws of war and just war theory, they would be justified, in many cases, in attempting revolution.[9] But we do not here call for revolution against the oppressors of the world; that would be a much different book. Instead, we argue in support of reimagining aspects of the liberal project so that it can provide a path forward for contemporary, deeply nonideal liberal societies. To borrow Juliet Hooker's apt phrasing, we need a fugitive politics of protest.[10] In our view, this requires reconciling the use of nonlethal violence with an understanding of protest as a particular kind of political communication that is borne out of, and grounded in, our political obligations to each other and our society.

In chapter 2, we consider the recent protests in Ferguson and Baltimore, and argue that nonlethal violence is sometimes communicatively required in protest when it is the only way to send a particular political message. The liberal ideal of protest as demanding change by civilly drawing attention to the inconsistencies between a society's sociopolitical ideals and its practices is just that, an ideal. It does not acknowledge the many difficulties faced by those trying to communicate publicly about the injustices they encounter to a majority that is in the grip of racist ideologies. Contra those who hold that violence is incompatible with political communication, we argue that violent protest is sometimes required for political communication because it can be the only way to break through the ideological blinders that block the majority from seeing the oppressive nature of their society. Moreover, there are circumstances wherein nonviolence would undermine, or directly contravene, the content of the particular message that protesters are trying to send. The communicative necessity of violence does not mean, though, that it is moral or pragmatic. We conclude chapter 2 with our first discussion of the moral and pragmatic constraints on violent protest.

We then turn our attention to an underlying, particularly destabilizing, problem in this violence/nonviolence debate: the problem of what counts as violence. Is property destruction violent? How about throwing milkshakes or shoes at politicians? What should we say about structural conditions that limit people's life expectancies and rights? Are those violent? After all, they cause more harm than a milkshake, even though the milkshake is more shocking. In chapter 3, we argue for a conception of violence that both tracks how ordinary people use the term and that attempts to resist ideological infection (i.e., that does not uncritically accept that black men's actions are always inherently violent, and that does not equate property destruction to personal injury). By considering carefully what violence is and is not, we draw out another of its distinctive communicative features, that it can be an effective mechanism for engendering humiliation. This helps us in the following chapter to determine how nonlethal violence might be used as a communicative tool in protest, given existing societal conditions.

Part of the usual rejection of interpersonal violent protest within traditional liberal domestic political theory is that such violence does not recognize its targets as fellow participants in the political sphere.[11] In chapter 4, we argue the opposite. Some communicative violence is consistent with regarding the targets of that violence as political co-participants. Insofar as violence can serve to shake the conceptual foundations of ideologies (chapter 2), to engender humiliation (chapter 3) that leads to new moral perceptions and understandings, and to demand respect and recognition from others, it is an appropriate and sometimes necessary tool of moral suasion. Rather than being simply coercive, it is persuasive. In this way, such violence treats its targets as fellow political participants, not merely objects to be bludgeoned.

Just because interpersonal violent protest is sometimes communicative and persuasive though, does not yet mean that it is politically and morally permitted. In chapter 5, following Iris Marion Young, we accept that we have a political obligation to work to bring about justice within our society. This is a uniquely communicative obligation toward collective action, which grounds the permission to protest. But we cannot do just anything in service of these obligations; we have other political and moral commitments that constrain us in various ways. We maintain that these limit, but sometimes permit, violent protest. We begin exploring these limits in chapter 2; here, we continue the discussion, enriching our understanding of how we may and must act in response to contemporary liberal, deeply oppressive societies. We outline the conditions under which defensive violence in response to oppression is morally permitted. When such defensive violence is simultaneously shaped by our political obligation to communicate toward collective action, it is also protest.

At this point, we have established that some nonlethal violent protest is in principle permissible in contemporary liberal societies. As a practical matter though, we might think protesters have good reasons to avoid violence. We thus turn in chapter 6 to the pragmatics of political communication, with a focus on protesters themselves. The overarching goal of protest is to both draw attention to injustice(s) and motivate others to take up the cause of reform or change. So, protesters must have a plan for political communication. They must take into account the relevant communicative context(s), including the social meanings of their words and actions, and social-historical facts about the audience(s) in question. Of course, protesters do not have to get everything right; communication always involves a shared burden. The onus is not solely on protesters to ensure that their attempts at political communication are successful. When considering whether or not to use violence, protesters must simply account for its communicative benefits and burdens in the exact same way that they must in general consider their tactics before acting.

In chapter 7, we return to the Bulldozer Protests/Revolution to interrogate the line between protest and revolution. We maintain that protest and revolution are not distinguished by nonviolence and violence, respectively (as many maintain), but by their essential communicative characters. Protest is an attempt to communicate *with* those in power and other members of the society, while revolution is an attempt to communicate to others *about* those in power. As we have argued throughout, protest involves trying to forge a communicative connection with the governing institutions of a society and its members under incredibly difficult communicative circumstances. Protesters seek to engender mutual recognition, shared public reasoning about justice, and consensual reform and change. By contrast, revolutionaries seek to communicate to others the impossibility of such a communicative connection with the society's governing institutions, and hence the need for their nonconsensual change. This way of drawing the distinction between protest and revolution carves out room for other kinds of political activism to count as protest without abandoning the core tenets of the liberal project.

Undoubtedly, this book leaves many important questions about protest unanswered. It is a work of applied political philosophy and, as such, strives to both engage the relevant conceptual arguments and make practical recommendations for how we should approach perennial and timely questions regarding violent and nonviolent protests. This dual focus on conceptual clarity and normative recommendations may be frustrating for some readers—however, we view both aspects as necessary to our project. This book, in the end, does not provide justification for any particular act of violent protest. Rather, it forges a new path forward for nonideal theorizing about protest in the "unjust meantime" in which we live.[12] We must move beyond the highly idealized model of protest as a public, conscientious, scrupulously nonviolent mode of political address, and instead conceptualize it as it is in the actual world: a full-throated, last-ditch effort to remedy serious, substantial injustices and oppressions without going to war.

NOTES

1. *Bringing Down a Dictator,* Documentary, directed by Steve York (New York: PBS, 2002).

2. Gene Sharp and Joshua Paulson, *Waging Nonviolent Struggle: 20th Century Practice and 21st Century Potential* (New York: Extending Horizons Books, 2005).

3. Kenya Evelyn, "Capitol Attack: The Five People Who Died," *The Guardian*, January 8, 2021.

4. Bill Chappell, "Architect of the Capitol Outlines $30 Million in Damages from Pro-Trump Riot," *NPR,* February 24, 2021.

5. Evelyn, "Capitol Attack: The Five People Who Died."

6. What it is for something to be a liberal society is complicated. It is also difficult to say what counts as reasonable. We go into more detail regarding these issues in chapter 1.

7. Kimberley Brownlee, *Conscience and Conviction: The Case for Civil Disobedience* (Oxford: Oxford University Press, 2012), 280.

8. Brownlee, *Conscience and Conviction: The Case for Civil Disobedience*, 280.

9. Christopher J. Finlay, *Terrorism and the Right to Resist: A Theory of Just Revolutionary War* (New York: Cambridge University Press, 2017).

10. Juliet Hooker, "Black Lives Matter and the Paradoxes of U.S. Black Politics: From Democratic Sacrifice to Democratic Repair," *Political Theory* 44, no. 4 (2016), 448–69.

11. Sally J. Scholz, "Political Solidarity and Violent Resistance," *Journal of Social Philosophy* 38, no. 1 (2007), 38–52.

12. Alison M. Jaggar, "Thinking about Justice in the Unjust Meantime," *Feminist Philosophy Quarterly* 5, no. 2 (2019).

BIBLIOGRAPHY

Bringing Down a Dictator. Documentary. Directed by York, Steve. New York: PBS, 2002.

Brownlee, Kimberley. *Conscience and Conviction: The Case for Civil Disobedience*. Oxford: Oxford University Press, 2012.

Chappell, Bill. "Architect of the Capitol Outlines $30 Million in Damages from Pro-Trump Riot." *NPR,* February 24, 2021. https://www.npr.org/sections/insurrection-at-the-capitol/2021/02/24/970977612/architect-of-the-capitol-outlines-30-million-in-damages-from-pro-trump-riot.

Evelyn, Kenya. "Capitol Attack: The Five People Who Died." *The Guardian,* January 8, 2021. http://www.theguardian.com/us-news/2021/jan/08/capitol-attack-police-officer-five-deaths.

Finlay, Christopher J. *Terrorism and the Right to Resist: A Theory of just Revolutionary War*. New York: Cambridge University Press, 2017.

Hooker, Juliet. "Black Lives Matter and the Paradoxes of U.S. Black Politics: From Democratic Sacrifice to Democratic Repair." *Political Theory* 44, no. 4 (2016): 448–469.

Jaggar, Alison M. "Thinking about Justice in the Unjust Meantime." *Feminist Philosophy Quarterly* 5, no. 2 (2019).

Scholz, Sally J. "Political Solidarity and Violent Resistance." *Journal of Social Philosophy* 38, no. 1 (2007): 38–52.

Sharp, Gene and Joshua Paulson. *Waging Nonviolent Struggle: 20th Century Practice and 21st Century Potential*. New York: Extending Horizons Books, 2005.

Chapter 1

A Brief (Philosophical) History of Protest and Liberalism

Thirty members of the Black Panther Party, openly carrying guns, entered the California state capitol building on May 2, 1967. They made their way to the back of the Assembly Chamber before being disarmed and led away by the police. This collective action was in response to the proposed California legislation that would forbid carrying a loaded weapon in public. The Black Panthers argued that this was a nonviolent protest, but when California governor Ronald Reagan signed the bill, he said that it would prevent the kind of violence seen in the capitol building earlier that year.[1] Was the Black Panthers' action violent? Was it protest?

The current liberal conceptual landscape draws clear distinctions between conscientious objection or refusal, legal protest, civil disobedience, and revolution. These distinctions are commonly determined by what theorists working in the liberal tradition take to be our moral and political rights and limitations within a liberal society.[2] In this chapter we demonstrate that such idealized theories of political protest cannot make sense of the Black Panthers' action without falling prey to serious definitional problems and deep concerns about justice in our imperfect world. We need a contemporary, nonideal theory of protest that can make sense of the Black Panthers' action, and others like it, as a case of political protest, despite its ostensibly violent (or at least threatening) nature.

COMMON LIBERAL CATEGORIES OF
RESISTANCE AND PROTEST

In the liberal tradition, there are a number of ways of talking about political resistance and protest. Conscientious objection or refusal is when an individual or group objects to and refuses to comply with some law, policy, or procedure on the basis of their strongly held convictions. The political right to conscientious objection or refusal is most commonly grounded in the moral right of conscience. As Kimberley Brownlee says, we have a "limited moral right of conscientious action as our expression of our conscientious convictions."[3] Muhammed Ali refusing to sign up for the Vietnam Draft is an oft-cited case of conscientious objection or refusal.

Legal protest is when an individual or group publicly communicates their disagreement—in a way that does not break the law—with some particular law, policy, procedure, institution, or political figure. Legal protestors contend publicly that the figure, institution, law, policy, or procedure in question does not align with their society's proclaimed moral, social, and political values and ideals, and so must be changed or removed. The political right to protest is most commonly grounded in the same moral right of conscience, combined with the moral rights of freedom of speech and action. Colin Kaepernick kneeling during the U.S. national anthem is an example of legal protest. There are no civil or criminal laws in the U.S. surrounding personal behavior during the playing of the national anthem (although there are in other countries). Kaepernick publicly communicated that his kneeling is a protest against systemic racism and police brutality, and his quintessentially public, communicative actions sparked a worldwide protest movement within professional and amateur athletics.

Civil disobedience is protest, except that, like conscientious objection, it breaks civil or criminal laws in the process of protesting. It seeks to publicly communicate a mismatch between a society's social and political practices and its proclaimed moral, social, and political values and ideals, and calls for change. Often, civil disobedience is grounded in those same moral rights of conscience and freedom of speech and action, as well as the moral right (or duty) to resist oppression.[4] As Martin Luther King, Jr., famously writes, "Oppressed people cannot remain oppressed forever. The urge for freedom will eventually come."[5]

Classic examples of civil disobedience include marching without a permit and illegal sit-ins/die-ins/occupations.

The question of what constitutes the "civil" aspect of civil disobedience is contested. Theorists have discussed it in terms of all of the following: politeness, general fidelity to law, a commitment to the shared political project, respect, a willingness to engage with others, and nonviolence.[6] For our part, we regard these debates as something of a red herring. Either civility equates to something like nonviolence, in which case we disagree that all protests must be civil (the aim of this book is to argue that violent protest is sometimes permitted), or it equates to something like a commitment to continuing to live in political community with others, in which case we agree that all protests must be civil. A protest need not be polite in the everyday sense of the term; to require this is to misunderstand the function of a protest, which is to communicate about injustice to those who may not be initially inclined to hear. However, if politeness means publicly communicative, then yes, protest must be civil. The issue of "civility" in protest thus dissolves into other, more fundamental questions, which we discuss throughout. It is in part to avoid these confusions that we prefer the term "protest" or "lawbreaking protest."

The distinction between objection or refusal and protest, while somewhat blurry in the actual world, is set sharply in liberal theory by the element of publicity. Conscientious objection or refusal can be a semi-private act known only to the individuals or groups objecting or refusing and to law enforcement agencies and other legal entities within the society. By contrast, protest—both legal and illegal—is a public act, that seeks to speak to the society at large.[7] Conscientious objection or refusal may be communicative, while protest is essentially communicative, and both are constrained, according to the liberal tradition, by the limitations of the moral rights and obligations that permit them in the first place.

Ideally, traditional liberal theorists claim, the laws, policies, and procedures regulating resistance and protest in liberal societies will at least loosely follow the moral permissions and constraints in play. As Ronald Dworkin puts it, "The debate [about rights to resist and protest] does not include the issue of whether citizens have *some* moral rights against their Government. It seems accepted on all sides that they do."[8] The debates are about which rights and duties citizens have, and which of those should be enshrined in law.

With respect to this second debate, one issue is how far laws, policies, and procedures can stray from determined moral permissions and duties in order to promote other key liberal political values such as stability, efficiency, and social utility. As John Rawls dryly notes, laws must work in the real world, and that is likely to require some departure from the ideal.[9] As a result, there are near-constant legal battles about resistance and protest within actual liberal societies. Just consider the judicial history of freedom of speech in the United States.

For the most part, going forward, we avoid consideration of such legal battles and issues. Our goal is to put forward a political theory of protest. While careful legal distinctions are essential in some contexts, they can lead political theorizing astray, insofar as such legalist concerns focus on parsing the law rather than on presenting a holistic political picture. We are concerned to provide a general political theory of protest that is apt for seriously nonideal, yet ostensibly liberal societies, and so leave the (necessary) legal discussions for another day.

Where there is general agreement amidst these debates is with respect to the necessity of nonviolence. Violent political acts, many liberal theorists argue, *cannot count* as conscientious objection or refusal and protest, either because violence is not communicative, or because it is morally prohibited, or because it constitutes a denial of the liberal project of political engagement via persuasion and not force. Once a certain level of violence is present,[10] we are out of the realm of protest and into the realm of either individual defense or war. Importantly, liberalism does not always condemn violence—the rights of self- and other-defense permit, if not require, violence in certain circumstances,[11] as do the rights of rebellion and revolution against tyranny.[12] Rather, the common—though not universal—claim is that political violence *within domestic society* just isn't protest.

This claim is also made by members of the general public. There is an almost knee-jerk response that violent protest is never justified, and probably is not protest at all. This occurs despite the fact that many liberal societies take great pride in their historical origins in violent resistance, rebellion, and revolution against oppression and tyranny. There are of course a myriad of questions we could ask about the acceptance of this apparent contradiction; however, we leave the psychology of cognitive dissonance for the relevant experts. Our goal is to refute the claim that violent protest is anathema to the liberal project.

Finally, in carving up these categories, note that protest, conscientious refusal or objection, and other nonviolent and violent political actions, can all be lumped together under the concept of resistance. Thinking in terms of resistance, rather than protest, can be helpful for discerning the nature of both individual and group actions. Resistance has the benefit of being a broad category; as Tamara Fakhoury has argued, there are many different ways in which a person can resist.[13] However, protest and resistance are not co-extensive. While protest functions as a kind of resistance, it is possible to engage in resistance that is not protest—either because it is not communicative, or it is not public, or it is not conscientious, among other possibilities.[14] Protest is demarcated more narrowly by its public communicative character, its conscientiousness, and typically its nonviolence. We intend to carve out a space for violence within protest in particular, rather than resistance more broadly, because violence has distinctive communicative characteristics that should not be overlooked.

PRESSING THE LIBERAL TRADITION

Many theorists have argued that the liberal tradition is morally, socially, and politically bankrupt. Citing systemic oppression, they argue that we ought to abandon the liberal project altogether, and instead view contemporary resistance and protest primarily through the lens of defense, rebellion, and revolution. From Karl Marx[15] to Frantz Fanon[16] to Chad Kautzer,[17] the radical or progressive tradition maintains that liberalism, in both principle and practice, essentially depends on the maintenance of a permanent underclass, which is structurally disempowered, exploited, and oppressed. Overthrowing this fundamentally unjust divide will require overthrowing liberalism itself; reform—of the kind often called for by protest in liberal societies—will not do the trick. If such a fundamental restructuring of society can be achieved nonviolently, so much the better. But if violence is required, it is permitted, because liberal societies (in this view) are at their cores oppressive and tyrannical.

According to this picture, all protest is a precursor to revolution. It is a shot across the bow, a warning that revolution is coming if those in power do not accede to the protesters' demands. As Malcolm X famously said, "It'll be ballots, or it'll be bullets. It'll be liberty, or it will be death. The only difference about this kind of death—it'll be reciprocal."[18] The radical or progressive tradition does not view violence as fundamentally incompatible with protest, given its classification of protest as just one type of defense against tyranny and oppression. By contrast, the liberal tradition is likely to regard such political violence as rebellion, insurrection, or revolution, but not as protest.

This might seem to be a dispute over words—one person's protest is another person's revolution. However, the dispute goes much deeper than that: it gets at the core of what we owe—morally, communicatively, pragmatically, politically—to all those disparate other people and groups with whom we live. What may we do to change, and maintain, and fix, and rebuild, our sociopolitical worlds? The liberal tradition claims that a continued commitment to living together in a reasonably just society demands public, conscientious, communicative, nonviolent protest.[19] The radical tradition claims that bringing about a just society out of what we currently have allows violence, because when you are fighting for your and your compatriots' freedom against tyranny and oppression, (almost) anything goes.[20]

Contemporary ostensibly liberal societies contain large and serious amounts of oppression.[21] Moreover, as Charles Mills argues, it is not merely that these societies happen to be oppressive; rather, it is that liberalism, as practiced in the real world, is built on the oppression of those people classified as nonwhite. As he writes, Western liberalism enshrines nonwhite subpersonhood simultaneously with white personhood; the rise of contemporary liberalism, as a historical reality, is based on a racial contract between whites to exclude persons of color from the group to whom political equality should apply.[22] The liberal polity that arose in the eighteenth and nineteenth centuries was "in fact a racial one, a white-supremacist state, for which differential white racial entitlement and nonwhite racial subordination were defining, thus inevitably molding white moral psychology and moral theorizing."[23] Racism, then, is not simply "a regrettable deviation from the ideal" of social contract liberalism, but rather "adherence to the actual norm" inherent in the system, which says to treat whites and nonwhites differently, because whites are persons and nonwhites are subpersons.[24] As Mills concludes, this racially differentiated designation of personhood status is how an "antipatriarchalist Enlightenment liberalism, with its proclamations of the equal rights, autonomy, and freedom of all men," is squared or reconciled with "the massacre, expropriation, and subjection to hereditary slavery of men at least apparently human."[25]

This racial encoding at the core of Western liberalism's history as an actual political practice means that, as Toni Morrison argues, Americanness definitionally means whiteness. American white self-conceptions, and many European white self-conceptions, are bound up with *not being* the black Other, with *not being* a subperson who is cognitively, morally, and emotionally inferior.[26] This conception persists, though the "social contract has been formally extended to apply to everyone, so that 'persons' is no longer coextensive with 'whites.'"[27] The dichotomy creates the illusion for whites that racism is no longer a problem, precisely because liberalism's focus on formal equality encourages whites to dismiss the ways in which several hundred years of racial privilege have configured material and power inequities in ways that fundamentally structure a person's life and life chances.[28] As Patricia Williams puts it, contemporary liberalism contains a kind of "racism in drag" that masquerades among whites in the form of the idea that the status quo is somehow neutral, that it is a natural baseline from which we should work, and not the product of centuries of colonization, discrimination, and oppression.[29] These crucial realities are ignored because they are nonideal.

Given the ways that liberalism in practice works to produce and maintain white ignorance of racial privilege and oppression, it might seem that to overcome oppression and structural injustice, we must discard liberalism as a political project. Crucially, those who would call merely for liberal reform fail to recognize that it is nearly impossible for nonwhites to protest their oppression in a way that will be recognized as persuasive by the white majority. This is partially because, following Miranda Fricker, nonwhites in liberal societies are victims of epistemic injustice. In the eyes of their broader political community, they lack credibility, testimonial expertise, and interpretive authority, and so are neither to be listened to nor trusted when they speak about and describe their experiences, especially their experiences of oppression.[30] Linking Fricker's point to Mills' analysis, we can conclude that liberalism has the silencing of nonwhite groups built into itself. Given this, how can nonwhites successfully protest, in the liberal mode, in contemporary societies?

In practice, liberalism seems to cut anti-racist protest off at the knees. The conceptual resources it traditionally provides for protest—conscientiousness, publicity, political engagement via moral suasion, public reason, and a commitment to nonviolence—depend on there being a rough epistemic parity between groups, such that political communication is a matter of drawing attention to and describing problems of injustice using more-or-less shared understandings and conceptions. But much as men cannot hear women when they are angry, so too whites cannot hear persons of color when they protest structural racism. The epistemic oppression to which persons of color are subject makes it so that the relevant understandings and conceptions are both *not* shared and are unlikely to be taken up by those in a position of privilege. Thus, sometimes, engaging in protest in the liberal mode is an exercise in futility: it is baring one's burdens to the blank, perpetually uncomprehending eyes of the privileged, who simply do not—and in many cases cannot, given their structurally manufactured white ignorance—understand what there is to complain about.

Liberalism is also accused of silencing oppressed groups by restricting the realm of political deliberation to those discussions that can take place using the language and concepts of shared public reason. Rawls argues that in public discourse about "fundamental political questions," citizens should leave their comprehensive doctrines of the good life at the door.[31] They should use only *reasonable* reasons and arguments, that is, those reasons and arguments that other citizens, conceptualized as "free and equal in a system of social cooperation over generations," could be expected to understand and accept.[32] This criterion of reasonableness structures public political debate and limits its content. Structurally, only arguments framed reasonably can be presented and content-wise, only arguments that "offer one another fair terms of cooperation" even at "the cost of their own interests" are acceptable entries.[33] Liberalism thus blocks some issues from being considered as valid topics for political discourse on the basis that they do not fall within the sphere of shared public reason.

For example, the fight for women's rights tends to involve women pointing out that there are particular problems that affect them uniquely that their society as a whole needs to address. But liberalism disregards, as a matter of principle, particular reasons unless they can be translated into public reasons; thus, feminists are either silenced or forced to engage in disingenuous argumentation. As Ajume Wingo points out, "by positing a single mode of public discourse, the [liberal] account of public reason forces individuals to trim and tailor their expression to the point that the reasons they give for a conclusion are literally not their own."[34] If they fail to do this—if women insist that the oppressions they face are not translatable to reasons that abstract free and equal citizens in a system of shared cooperation could find relatable, if not compelling—then they are simply dismissed as unreasonable, as trying to smuggle "illiberal commitments" into the public sphere.[35] So, the ongoing fight for women's rights in contemporary liberal societies is dismissed as a "women's issue."

Because liberalism is neutral on conceptions of the good life, it maintains the public sphere as a space for discussion of only those common interests that all people in a society could be reasonably said to share. In societies marred by pervasive injustice, imposing this liberal principle has the effect of silencing oppressed groups, because they do not share the so-called reasonable common interests of the majority. Their differential social positioning means that privileged groups and oppressed groups have very different interests in practice, such that calls for justice by the oppressed are likely, if not inevitably, to be read as illiberal by the privileged. For instance, in the United States, many conservatives and otherwise progressive members of privileged groups deride calls for speech restrictions as fundamentally illiberal, despite oppressed groups explaining that some speech is deeply harmful.[36] So even when the majority can overcome their ignorance enough to hear the oppressed, they are likely to dismiss the concerns raised as falling outside the scope of, if not undermining, justice.

Liberalism in the context of oppression silences groups in at least two ways. These silencings are connected; they form a feedback loop that, in concert with the standard liberal constraints on protest, makes it extraordinarily difficult for oppressed groups to successfully engage in protest and bring about real change in their social and political relations. The ties of community are what make the notion of shared public reason appropriate, but when the privileged groups within a society cannot hear oppressed groups, this both demonstrates that those ties of community are frayed, and frays and breaks them further.[37] The lack of communal ties, in turn, reduces the space of shared public reason, because where there are no ties of community, there are no, or very few, reasonable common interests around which a society as a whole can gather. And this reduction of the space of shared public reason makes it even more difficult for privileged groups to take seriously the concerns of the oppressed, thus reinforcing privileged groups' tendencies to not be able to hear the oppressed at all.[38] So the feedback loop continues, made worse by liberalism's requirements that protestors be civil, conscientious, and nonviolent at all times. Liberalism functionally makes protests into complaint societies for oppressed groups in particular, ones that are continually ignored. This enables, if not encourages, pervasive injustice to continue.

MOVING FORWARD: REIMAGINING LIBERALISM

The question is how to break out of this feedback loop. Perhaps we should leave liberalism behind as a relic of colonizer thinking.[39] Those who call for wholesale revolution make this move; they argue that the only way to overcome oppression is a fundamental restructuring of society on the basis of radical, rather than liberal, principles.[40] However, we maintain that the liberal project, if reimagined in certain ways, can provide a political theory of protest appropriate for our world. The core element of liberalism that we wish to hold on to is the idea that people can have societies that make progress toward justice equally enjoyed by all via moral suasion and argumentation, without imposing substantive moral ideals or notions of the good life on their members.[41] In such societies, which we maintain are worth fighting to have and keep, protest is permitted so long as it is a tool of persuasion and not force.

For such protest to work, though, it cannot remain fettered to all of traditional liberalism's process, structural, and content constraints. Theorists have argued that a number of these constraints are not actually entailed by the core of the liberal project. Candice Delmas contends that one way of breaking the silencing of oppressed groups is to engage in uncivil disobedience: civility, contrary to common opinion, is not actually required in the face of serious injustice.[42] Brownlee maintains that protest only needs to be conscientious—it need not be either civil or necessarily nonviolent, or even public.[43] N. P. Adams concludes that some property destruction is compatible with protest.[44] We argue that protest need not be nonviolent, and that certain forms of nonlethal interpersonal violence may be communicatively required for protest, even in a liberal society. Such nonlethal violent protest is one (heretofore mostly neglected) way of breaking the aforementioned feedback loop without abandoning the project of persuasion in favor of force and engaging in wholesale revolution.

There are at least three reasons for avoiding the revolutionary path. First, the oppressions that plague contemporary liberal societies are structural; so, the solutions must attack the relevant societal structures, rather than the particular individuals and groups who hold power. Insofar as revolutions primarily aim to change who holds power in a society, they may or may not involve the structural shifts necessary to overcome oppression. A revolution may occur, and then re-inscribe the precise oppressions that previously existed within a society, though perhaps in an altered form. Consider the French Revolution: while the monarchy was indeed overthrown, the Terror that came afterward reproduced classism and sexism. The American Revolution fought for freedom from Great Britain, but in the process, further entrenched American chattel slavery.

Second, because the problems are structural, revolutions are morally suspect insofar as they target particular individuals. But those individuals are not necessarily liable for the structural problems that exist. This is because it is part of the nature of structural problems that no one individual is morally responsible—in a way that makes them liable— for them.[45] Structural problems are properly understood as emerging from collective actions over time, rather than as the particular immoral actions of evil individuals.[46] The upshot is that, if the goal of a revolution is to justly attack the oppressive societal structures, it will have to do so without targeting particular individuals. But part of the nature of revolutions in practice is that they do target particular individuals and groups in an attempt to reconfigure who has power in a society. The two intertwined concerns here are that revolutions either won't attack the relevant oppressive structures or will try to do so by targeting particular individuals, which is itself unjust because those individuals aren't liable. It may be possible for revolutions to be fought justly, but given our nonideal conditions and the nature of structural oppression, it is certainly improbable.

The final reason for avoiding revolution is practical. In revolutions, lots of people are killed or die, and many more are seriously injured, physically, socially, and psychologically.[47] And furthermore, many of the killed, dead, and injured are innocent in the sense of not being liable for the injustices at issue. Although she notes that the statistical data is difficult to parse (in part because it is incomplete and in part because statistical methodological issues abound) international legal theorist and historian Valerie Epps concludes that civilian deaths have far outnumbered military deaths in the past two centuries, and may continue to do so, given the nature of modern warfare.[48] Revolutions, like all wars in practice, do not discriminate; that is, they do not successfully distinguish between who is liable to be intentionally targeted in warfare, and who is not. Revolutions especially have a tendency, historically speaking, to be particularly vicious.[49] Given these costs, we are wary, as Lionel McPherson puts it, of putting "blind faith in the value of 'doing something' by killing, and killing some more."[50] Widespread killing doesn't lead to justice; hard work at the negotiating table is what leads to justice.[51]

If revolution ought to be avoided, we must seek an alternative way of breaking the silencing feedback loop built into liberalism in practice. We consider protest as a political phenomenon that occurs within liberal societies. Hence, it is not grounded solely in baseline moral appeals, but rather in the invariable combination of moral and political realities. The personal is political, and the political is personal.[52] Many people today live under conditions of serious oppression, and yet take themselves to have (and perhaps really do have) political obligations to both their society and its members. Given these conditions and obligations, people can do more, protest-wise, than has generally been accepted in traditional liberal political theory.

In this vein, perhaps the Black Panthers' political action at the California statehouse in 1967 was an act of political communication, one taken in order to get their message across in the face of widespread silencing. It sent a complicated series of political messages about power, community defense, and race relations in the United States. It may not be a "comfortable" protest, especially to whites who are accustomed to having their voices heard in the first instance. But black Americans attempting to communicate about oppression in a society designed to suppress and ignore them is never going to be comfortable. The Black Panthers' actions that day may not have been as scrupulous as traditional liberalism would like, but they were, despite their ostensibly violent nature, publicly and politically communicative.

NOTES

1. Adam Winkler, "The Secret History of Guns," *The Atlantic*, September 2011.

2. Joseph Raz, *The Authority of Law: Essays on Law and Morality* (Oxford: Oxford University Press, 1979), 304.

3. Kimberley Brownlee, *Conscience and Conviction: The Case for Civil Disobedience* (Oxford: Oxford University Press, 2012), 7.

4. N.P. Adams grounds civil disobedience in a commitment to the political, rather than a moral right. We discuss his view in depth in chapter 4. N. P. Adams, "Uncivil Disobedience: Political Commitment and Violence," *Res Publica* 24 (2018), 475–91.

5. Martin Luther King Jr., "A Letter from Birmingham Jail," *The Atlantic Monthly 212.2*, August 1963.

6. For a good overview of the debates surrounding civility, see Candice Delmas, "Civil Disobedience," *Philosophical Compass* 11, no. 11 (2016), 681–91.

7. Bob Pepperman Taylor, *The Routledge Guidebook to Thoreau's Civil Disobedience* (London: Taylor & Francis Group, 2014).

8. Ronald Dworkin, *Taking Rights Seriously* (Cambridge, MA: Harvard University Press, 1977), 92.

9. John Rawls, *A Theory of Justice, Revised Edition* (Cambridge, MA: Belknap Press, 1999), Preface.

10. Opinions differ here. For some theorists, any violence, whether against property or persons, is incompatible with protest, while others draw the line at interpersonal violence.

11. Judith Jarvis Thomson, "Self-Defense," *Philosophy & Public Affairs* 20, no. 4 (1991), 283–310.

12. Michael Walzer, *Just and Unjust Wars: A Moral Argument with Historical Illustrations, Fourth Edition* (New York: Basic Books, 1977), 51–58, 89.

13. Tamara Fakhoury, "Dimensions of Resistance," in *Pacifism, Politics, and Feminism: Intersections and Innovations*, ed. Jennifer Kling (Leiden; Boston: Brill Rodopi, 2019), 68–79.

14. Tamara Fakhoury, "Quiet Resistance: The Value of Personal Defiance," *The Journal of Ethics* 25 (2021), 1–20.

15. Karl Marx, Friedrich Engels and Frederic L. Bender, *The Communist Manifesto*, 2nd ed. (New York, NY: W.W. Norton & Co, 2013).

16. Frantz Fanon, *The Wretched of the Earth*, 1st Evergreen ed. (New York: Grove Weidenfeld, 1991).

17. Chad Kautzer, ed., *Radical Philosophy: An Introduction*, 1st Edition ed. (New York: Routledge, 2015).

18. Malcolm X, "The Ballot or the Bullet," in *The Radical Reader*, eds. Timothy Patrick McCarthy and John McMillian (New York: The New Press, 2003), 382–89.

19. The nature of each of these conditions is subject to deep debate, and their relative importance and primacy is disputed in the literature. However, liberal theorists do agree that, so long as a society is more-or-less reasonably just, widespread political violence is ruled out.

20. Scott Crow, "Liberatory Community Armed Self-Defense," in *Setting Sights: Histories and Reflections on Community Armed Self-Defense*, ed. Scott Crow (California: PM Press, 2017), 7–13.There is serious disagreement among radical/progressive theorists as to the amount and kinds of violence that may be used to bring about justice. Although a very few radical/progressive theorists advocate total war, the majority maintain that standard just war prohibitions apply to defensive political violence. Chad Kautzer, "Notes for a Critical Theory of Community Self-Defense," in *Setting Sights: Histories and Reflections on Community Armed Self-Defense*, ed. Scott Crow (Oakland, CA: PM Press, 2017), 35–48.

21. See, among others, Michelle Alexander, Angela Davis, Elizabeth Anderson, Kimberlé Crenshaw, Alison Jaggar, Miranda Fricker, Brittney Cooper, Ann Cudd, Tommie Shelby, Lucius Outlaw, and Joanna Kadi.

22. Charles W. Mills, *The Racial Contract* (Ithaca, NY: Cornell University Press, 1997), chapter 1.

23. Mills, *The Racial Contract*, 57.

24. Mills, *The Racial Contract*, 56.

25. Mills, *The Racial Contract*, 64.

26. Toni Morrison, *Playing in the Dark: Whiteness and the Literary Imagination* (Cambridge: Harvard University Press, 1992).

27. Mills, *The Racial Contract*, 73.

28. Mills, *The Racial Contract*, 73–76.

29. Patricia J. Williams, *The Alchemy of Race and Rights* (Cambridge: Harvard University Press, 1991), 116.

30. Miranda Fricker, *Epistemic Injustice: Power and the Ethics of Knowing* (Oxford: Oxford University Press, 2007).

31. John Rawls, "The Idea of Public Reason Revisited," *The University of Chicago Law Review* 64, no. 3 (1997), 132.

32. Rawls, "The Idea of Public Reason Revisited," 132–36.

33. Rawls, "The Idea of Public Reason Revisited," 136.

34. Ajume Wingo, "Modes of Public Reasoning in the Islamic/West Debate," Presented at the October 2005 meeting of the Malta Forum, Casablanca, Morocco (2005), 10.

35. Marilyn Friedman, "John Rawls and the Political Coercion of Unreasonable People," in *Autonomy, Gender, Politics* (Oxford: Oxford University Press, 2003), 17.

36. Barrett Emerick, "The Limits of the Rights to Free Thought and Expression," *Kennedy Institute of Ethics Journal* 31, no. 2 (2021), 133–52.

37. Candice Delmas, *A Duty to Resist: When Disobedience Should Be Uncivil* (New York, NY: Oxford University Press, 2018), 65.

38. As Candice Delmas writes, "What ties of community are there if the majority cannot bring itself to hear oppressed minorities even when they follow

all of the strictures of civility?" Delmas, *A Duty to Resist: When Disobedience Should Be Uncivil*, 65.

39. Barbara Arneil, "Liberal Colonialism, Domestic Colonies and Citizenship," *History of Political Thought* 33, no. 3 (2012), 491–523.

40. Lisa H. Schwartzman, *Challenging Liberalism: Feminism as Political Critique* (Pennsylvania: Pennsylvania State University Press, 2006).

41. This is not a defense of neoliberalism; it is a defense of progressivism, which Charles Mills argues is the actual core of the liberal project. As he says, liberal societies needn't hold to traditional racial liberalism; they could move to progressive liberalism instead, and have the theoretical constructs in place to do so. Daniel Steinmetz-Jenkins, "Charles Mills Thinks Liberalism Still has a Chance," *The Nation*, January 28, 2021.

42. Delmas, *A Duty to Resist: When Disobedience should be Uncivil*.

43. Brownlee, *Conscience and Conviction: The Case for Civil Disobedience*.

44. Adams, "Uncivil Disobedience: Political Commitment and Violence," 475–91.

45. For more on structural problems and responsibility, see chapter 5.

46. See, among others, Iris Marion Young, "Five Faces of Oppression," in *Justice and the Politics of Difference* (New Jersey: Princeton University Press, 1990a), 39–65; Marilyn Frye, "Oppression," in *The Politics of Reality* (New York: Crossing Press, 1983), 1–16; Sally Haslanger, "Oppressions: Racial and Other," in *Racism in Mind*, eds. Michael P. Levine and Tamas Pataki (Ithaca: Cornell University Press, 2004), 97–123. Of course, agent-oppression is possible, and indeed likely, in oppressive societies; but it is not necessary for continued oppression.

47. Erica Chenoweth and Maria J. Stephan, *Why Civil Resistance Works: The Strategic Logic of Nonviolent Conflict* (New York: Columbia University Press, 2011).

48. Valerie Epps, "Civilian Casualties in Modern Warfare: The Death of the Collateral Damage Rule," *Georgia Journal of International and Comparative Law* 41, no. Winter 2013 (2011), 11–39.

49. Christopher J. Finlay, *Terrorism and the Right to Resist: A Theory of just Revolutionary War* (New York: Cambridge University Press, 2017).

50. Lionel K. McPherson, "The Costs of Violence: Militarism, Geopolitics, and Accountability," in *To Shape a New World: Essays on the Political Philosophy of Martin Luther King, Jr*, eds. Tommie Shelby and Brandon M. Terry (Cambridge, MA: Harvard University Press, 2018), 266.

51. In any particular instance, some warfare may be necessary to bring the relevant groups to the negotiating table; we do not maintain an anti-war pacifist position. However, given the horrors of war, it is essential to try all other avenues before contemplating revolution. This book is an argument for one such avenue.

52. Iris Marion Young, *Justice and the Politics of Difference* (Princeton, NJ: Princeton University Press, 1990b).

BIBLIOGRAPHY

Adams, N. P. "Uncivil Disobedience: Political Commitment and Violence." *Res Publica* 24, (2018): 475–491.

Arneil, Barbara. "Liberal Colonialism, Domestic Colonies and Citizenship." *History of Political Thought* 33, no. 3 (2012): 491–523.

Brownlee, Kimberley. *Conscience and Conviction: The Case for Civil Disobedience.* Oxford: Oxford University Press, 2012.

Chenoweth, Erica and Maria J. Stephan. *Why Civil Resistance Works: The Strategic Logic of Nonviolent Conflict.* New York: Columbia University Press, 2011.

Crow, Scott. "Liberatory Community Armed Self-Defense." In *Setting Sights: Histories and Reflections on Community Armed Self-Defense*, edited by Scott Crow, 7–13. California: PM Press, 2017.

Delmas, Candice. "Civil Disobedience." *Philosophical Compass* 11, no. 11 (2016): 681–691.

———. *A Duty to Resist: When Disobedience should be Uncivil.* New York, NY: Oxford University Press, 2018.

Dworkin, Ronald. *Taking Rights Seriously.* Cambridge, MA: Harvard University Press, 1977.

Emerick, Barrett. "The Limits of the Rights to Free Thought and Expression." *Kennedy Institute of Ethics Journal* 31, no. 2 (2021): 133–52. https://philarchive.org.

Epps, Valerie. "Civilian Casualties in Modern Warfare: The Death of the Collateral Damage Rule." *Georgia Journal of International and Comparative Law* 41, no. Winter 2013 (2011): 11–39.

Fakhoury, Tamara. "Dimensions of Resistance." In *Pacifism, Politics, and Feminism: Intersections and Innovations*, edited by Kling, Jennifer, 68–79. Leiden; Boston: Brill Rodopi, 2019.

———. "Quiet Resistance: The Value of Personal Defiance." *The Journal of Ethics* 25 (2021): 1–20.

Fanon, Frantz. *The Wretched of the Earth.* 1st Evergreen ed. New York: Grove Weidenfeld, 1991.

Finlay, Christopher J. *Terrorism and the Right to Resist: A Theory of just Revolutionary War.* New York: Cambridge University Press, 2017.

Fricker, Miranda. *Epistemic Injustice: Power and the Ethics of Knowing.* Oxford: Oxford University Press, 2007.

Friedman, Marilyn. "John Rawls and the Political Coercion of Unreasonable People." In *Autonomy, Gender, Politics*, edited by Marilyn Friedman. Oxford: Oxford University Press, 2003.

Frye, Marilyn. "Oppression." In *The Politics of Reality*, edited by Marilyn Frye, 1–16. New York: Crossing Press, 1983.

Haslanger, Sally. "Oppressions: Racial and Other." In *Racism in Mind*, edited by Levine, Michael P. and Tamas Pataki, 97–123. Ithaca: Cornell University Press, 2004.

Kautzer, Chad. "Notes for a Critical Theory of Community Self-Defense." In *Setting Sights: Histories and Reflections on Community Armed Self-Defense*, edited by Crow, Scott, 35–48. Oakland, CA: PM Press, 2017.

———. *Radical Philosophy: An Introduction*. 1st Edition ed. New York: Routledge, 2015.

King Jr., Martin Luther. "A Letter from Birmingham Jail." *The Atlantic Monthly 212.2* (August 1963).

Malcolm X. "The Ballot or the Bullet." In *The Radical Reader*, edited by McCarthy, Timothy Patrick and John McMillian, 382–389. New York: The New Press, 2003.

Marx, Karl, Friedrich Engels, and Frederic L. Bender. *The Communist Manifesto*, 2nd ed. New York, NY: W.W. Norton & Co, 2013.

McPherson, Lionel K. "The Costs of Violence: Militarism, Geopolitics, and Accountability." In *To Shape a New World: Essays on the Political Philosophy of Martin Luther King, Jr*, edited by Shelby, Tommie and Brandon M. Terry, 253–266. Cambridge, MA: Harvard University Press, 2018.

Mills, Charles W. *The Racial Contract*. Ithaca, NY: Cornell University Press, 1997.

Morrison, Toni. *Playing in the Dark: Whiteness and the Literary Imagination*. Cambridge: Harvard University Press, 1992.

Rawls, John. "The Idea of Public Reason Revisited." *The University of Chicago Law Review* 64, no. 3 (1997): 765–807.

———. *A Theory of Justice, Revised Edition*. Cambridge, MA: Belknap Press, 1999.

Raz, Joseph. *The Authority of Law: Essays on Law and Morality*. Oxford: Oxford University Press, 1979.

Schwartzman, Lisa H. *Challenging Liberalism: Feminism as Political Critique*. Pennsylvania: Pennsylvania State University Press, 2006.

Steinmetz-Jenkins, Daniel. "Charles Mills Thinks Liberalism Still has a Chance." *The Nation* (January 28, 2021). https://www.thenation.com/article/culture/charles-mills-thinks-theres-still-time-to-rescue-liberalism/.

Taylor, Bob Pepperman. *The Routledge Guidebook to Thoreau's Civil Disobedience*. London: Taylor & Francis Group, 2014.

Thomson, Judith Jarvis. "Self-Defense." *Philosophy & Public Affairs* 20, no. 4 (1991): 283–310.

Walzer, Michael. *Just and Unjust Wars: A Moral Argument with Historical Illustrations, Fourth Edition.* New York: Basic Books, 1977.

Williams, Patricia J. *The Alchemy of Race and Rights.* Cambridge: Harvard University Press, 1991.

Wingo, Ajume. "Modes of Public Reasoning in the Islamic/West Debate." Presented at the October 2005 meeting of the Malta Forum, Casablanca, Morocco.

Winkler, Adam. "The Secret History of Guns." *The Atlantic,* September 2011. https://www.theatlantic.com/magazine/archive/2011/09/the-secret-history -of-guns/308608/.

Young, Iris Marion. "Five Faces of Oppression." In *Justice and the Politics of Difference,* 39–65. New Jersey: Princeton University Press, 1990a.

———. *Justice and the Politics of Difference.* Princeton, NJ: Princeton University Press, 1990b.

Chapter 2

Bottles and Bricks

Rethinking the Prohibition against Violent Protest

Freddie Gray, Jr., a twenty-five-year-old black man, died on April 25, 2015, from injuries sustained while in the custody of the Baltimore City Police.[1] In the wake of his death, protests that initially were almost, if not wholly, nonviolent took on a different character. In a series of incidents spanning approximately four days, civilians clashed with police, throwing bricks, bottles, and rocks. They set fire to buildings and vehicles, broke storefront windows, and stole from business establishments. People on all sides suffered injuries. The conflict culminated in Maryland Governor Larry Hogan declaring a state of emergency, imposing a curfew, and calling in the Maryland National Guard.

The individuals who took part in these lawbreaking activities were widely condemned by politicians and activists on the mainstream political right and left. Those on the right sought to associate the events with civil rights organizations like Black Lives Matter (BLM). The left painted the violent participants as opportunists who took advantage of the crowds and conditions to pursue an agenda separate from the peaceful protests.[2] Even those who acknowledged that the same conditions that gave rise to the protests were also responsible for the turmoil lamented the acts as harmful to local people and businesses.

President Obama went further. These acts, he claimed, were not only harmful and ineffective, but also inconsistent with the very nature of protest:

> [T]here's no excuse for the kind of violence that we saw yesterday. It is counterproductive. . . . When individuals get crowbars and start prying

19

open doors to loot, they're not protesting. They're not making a state-ment. They're stealing. When they burn down a building, they're com-mitting arson.[3]

In his condemnation, Obama invokes a common liberal conception of protest as a mode of address: it is a means of publicly articulating a message about perceived injustice. As such, protest is distinct both from revolutionary acts that seek to overturn the existing sociopolitical order and from rioting, which may be born of frustration with the sociopoliti-cal order, but is not intended as a political message.

On this view, lawbreaking political protests, often termed "civil disobedience," are permissible, but they are subject to limitations. One is a prohibition against violence, which often extends to a ban on the destruction of private property and theft.[4] Adherents of this view allow, and even applaud, when Martin Luther King, Jr. kneels in the streets without proper permits, but take a dim view of counter-demonstrators punching known neo-Nazis, even when their aim is to send a message about the threat neo-Nazis pose to the existing political order.[5]

As the latter example illustrates, not every violent act of protest is necessarily either revolutionary or riotous; so, the prohibition against violent protest must be justified on grounds other than the aims of the actors. Sometimes, it is grounded normatively. For example, one might argue that using violence as a communicative strategy is impermissible because doing so fails to respect others—it treats them as a mere means to sending a political message.[6] Sometimes, it is grounded pragmati-cally. Obama gestures at this when he calls violence "counterproduc-tive." The third argument against violent protest is conceptual. On this view, violence is inconsistent with political protest as a public com-municative effort in a liberal society.[7] Communication, in the public sphere, must meet certain standards, like an appeal to reason, which violence always fails. As Obama puts it, those who engage in violent lawbreaking are "not protesting. They're not making a statement." Though less commonly deployed in public discourse than pragmatic or moral critiques, this conceptual argument against violent protest is a powerful weapon in the liberal arsenal. It may amount to a denial that protesters, when they use violence to make their point, are communicat-ing at all.

In this chapter, we reject the conceptual argument against violence as protest through an examination of civilian responses to police brutality.

We follow Kimberley Brownlee, Candice Delmas, and others in asserting that (appropriately limited) violence is conceptually consistent with
protest as a mode of public address in a liberal society.[8] We then push
this argument further to show that violent protest may sometimes be
required to communicate about injustice. The injustice at the heart of
the Baltimore protests—namely, police brutality against black Americans—is a paradigmatic case of this sort, because of the particular
relationship of the police to both the injustice and the protests against
it. The violent acts of the Baltimore protesters (and similar events in
Ferguson) provide a starting point for thinking through violent protest
not merely as a political tactic but as, in some cases, a communicative
requirement.[9]

Of course, even when violent protest is communicatively required, it
is not yet justified; it must also be pragmatically effective and morally
permissible. We turn at the end of the chapter to the oft-cited moral and
pragmatic constraints on violence in protest to determine whether communicatively required violent protest might also meet these additional
criteria. We appeal to Juliet Hooker's work to help make sense of the
moral and pragmatic demands on black Americans protesting contemporary racial oppression.[10]

This chapter is not a backward-looking attempt to assess, defend,
praise, or blame the actions of the Baltimore and Ferguson protesters.
From what we know of how these events unfolded, people who took to
the streets and took up bottles, bricks, and the like did so for a variety
of reasons, from self-defense to frustration, and their acts may well
have been morally justified.[11] We draw on these events because (a) they
are recent instances in which the violence was (partially) condemned
through an appeal to the requirements of public communication; (b)
they are cases where the nature of the injustice has a particular structure; and (c) most importantly, they are quite literally inspiring, reveal-
ing communicative contours of our social milieu that were previously
obscured.

THE CONCEPTUAL ARGUMENT

The conceptual argument claims that violence is ruled out by the very
nature of protest as a public communicative effort. John Rawls, for
example, says violence is "incompatible with civil disobedience as

a mode of address."[12] In this section, we analyze and reject this conclusion. Conceptualizing lawbreaking protest as a mode of address grounds no communicative prohibition against violence. By contrast, violence is required for communication when it transmits a message about the nature of the injustice at issue that available forms of nonviolent protest are unable to send.

To begin, communication, broadly speaking, does not rule out the use of violence. Communicative acts can take a variety of forms, and not all are nonviolent. For example, killing the messenger is widely understood to indicate both extreme displeasure with the message received and a desire to end the conversation by eliminating the means of conversing. It is essentially communicative in that, in the paradigm case, it serves no further end and brings no tactical advantage. So, nonviolence cannot be a necessary condition of protest qua communicative act. Nor is nonviolence a necessary condition of the basic message of protesters that there is widespread injustice and a change is warranted. Burning a building or one's own body can send potentially powerful messages about injustice. As Brownlee writes,

> violence does not necessarily obscure the communicative quality of civil disobedience . . . [D]iscriminate, well-considered violent civil disobedience can provide an eloquent statement of both the dissenter's frustration and the importance of the issues he addresses. For these reasons, the use of violence can support rather than undermine . . . communicative aspects of civil disobedience.[13]

However, it might be that violence necessarily changes the relationship between the interlocutors. Protest is intended to persuade, rather than force. So, while violence is consistent with protest as a communicative act, it could be that it is communication of a fundamentally different kind insofar as it forces, rather than persuades. As Rawls understands it, lawbreaking protest is the last resort within the sphere of acceptable political discourse.[14] It should not take us out of that sphere and into one in which we try to force others to conform.

Notice though that not every act of violence forces. Self-immolation, mentioned above, is one example. Brownlee suggests that shooting into the air could fail Rawls' nonviolence proviso (since it risks injury or harm) without being forceful, threatening, or coercive.[15] And, many acts that are nonviolent are intended to (and do) force, threaten, or coerce.

An illegal teachers' strike produces no physical injury or harm but may be used to force legislatures to negotiate with union leadership.[16] If our goal is to preserve protest as a certain kind of communicative act grounded in values of public reason, then the onus is on those who would prohibit violence to show that all acts so classified violate those norms.[17]

It seems violence is, at least in some instances, consistent with protest as a communicative act aimed at resolving a serious injustice politically rather than via brute force. Nevertheless, it is worth wondering whether nonviolence might be essential to (part of) some message that must be conveyed in every act of protest. Think of the message that the protesters share a fundamental acceptance of the basic structure of society, its rules, values, and aspirations (as Rawls might put it, they have a general fidelity to law[18]), and wish to remain members of it. Such intentions are thought to be hallmarks of protest as opposed to revolution. But mere intentions are not enough. Some signal must be given. Perhaps nonviolence is required to convey the message of general fidelity to law and the desire to stay in the society.

Though we agree nonviolence may be *more likely* to communicate general fidelity to law and the desire to remain connected, it doesn't appear to be *essential* to sending this message. Imagine a violent vigilante who takes justice into her own hands to protect herself or others from a specific threat, and then immediately turns herself in and accepts punishment for her actions. While we might disapprove, we don't seriously question whether she is a generally law-abiding member of the community with a desire to remain connected to it; the peculiar character of her series of actions communicates that perfectly well.[19]

Furthermore, there are other circumstances wherein no matter how scrupulously the protesters adhere to nonviolence, their actions will be read as flouting the basic values and norms of society or as disrespecting the rule of law. Take the case of Colin Kaepernick kneeling for the national anthem. Here we have a member of an oppressed group who is not even engaging in a lawbreaking protest and yet is accused of violating core social values and of signaling a desire to break away from society.[20] This message is said to be transmitted by the way he chose to protest, in spite of Kaepernick's repeated attempts to communicate that his message is one that challenges the country to live up to its ideals, not one that challenges the content of those ideals. Nonviolence then, appears to be neither necessary nor always especially helpful in communicating fidelity to law and the desire to remain connected to the society.

If nonviolence is not necessary for the general communicative character of protest or its essential content, then it is not conceptually required by protest as a mode of address. However, nonviolence could still be integral to the message being sent in a particular case of law-breaking protest. Brownlee claims that, through lawbreaking, "a civil disobedient aims to lead policymakers not only to reform existing law, but also to internalise her objections so as to produce a lasting change in the law."[21] This suggests that protesters must respect certain norms of discourse, and so must constrain their use of violence to that which is "consistent with both the persuasive aims of civilly disobedient communication and a civil respect for their hearers."[22] But, viewed from another angle, it is a reminder that the means of protest may be selected not only to convey that an injustice is occurring or that it is serious, but also to communicate a message about the particular nature of the injustice at issue. In the wake of demonstrations and legal advocacy for civil rights and desegregation in the public sphere, lunch counter sit-ins were a potent illustration that, even when relegated to the policies of private businesses, segregationist policies violated the basic dignity of black Americans. Highlighting this, protesters sometimes responded to inquiries about their goals by stating that they "only wanted a cup of coffee" or "just wanted to eat."[23] Statements that captured such ordinary aspirations demonstrated the nature of the injustice in a way that infiltrating different whites-only spaces, like golf courses, might not. These moments invited white Americans to conceptualize the wrongs of racial segregation in ways that were not easily articulable by appeal to existing understandings of constitutional guarantees, and so contributed to a shift in the meaning of the principle of equality.[24]

The act of protest need not communicate anything about the particular nature of the injustice. Chaining oneself to a government building or blocking traffic are, in many instances, nonspecific acts of protest; they communicate nothing about the nature of the injustice, but seek only to direct attention to the protesters, so that they can deliver their message. Still, the choice between tactics is sometimes made on the basis of their various communicative qualities. And so, violent protest may be ruled out as a tactic on communicative grounds; specifically, it is ruled out when it would undermine a group's message about the nature of the injustice at issue. Imagine if Quakers were to protest a new law requiring them to register for the draft. Engaging in a nonviolent protest would be essential to their demonstration. Not only are they pacifists who oppose violence on moral grounds, but also the particular injustice that they are protesting is being forced to violate their pacifist beliefs. The use of violent protest would thus undercut, if not flatly contradict, their message. The constraints of public reason push the protesters not only to voice their concern but also to frame their message in a way that has internal coherence. In doing so, they communicate not merely reasonably, but rationally.

Just as the use of nonviolence may be required to communicate a group's message, the converse could obtain—consistency might require violence. Protests of any size, law-abiding or not, invite a police presence for the ostensive purpose of maintaining order. That law enforcement reliably performs this role allows the majority to square the permissibility of protest with a sense of security and a general expectation of respect for the rule of law. The ideal model of protest, on this view, is one in which police carefully monitor the situation, protecting nonviolent demonstrators, nonviolent counter-demonstrators, and the surrounding community.[25] Just as liberals demand that protest be done in such a way that it signals a general respect for law and order, they also demand that police provide a measured, controlled reaction to nonviolent protest. That this is the expectation was made clear by the conflicting responses to police actions at BLM protests during the summer of 2020. Those who saw the protesters as peaceful argued that police violence toward protesters was unwarranted. Others, who viewed the protesters as violent (or potentially violent), saw the police's use of force as justified.

This relationship between law enforcement and protest, in most instances, does not greatly affect protesters in their efforts to communicate and may even provide the necessary support for those communicative efforts. But sometimes, it undercuts a vital message about a central feature of the relevant injustice by conveying contradictory information. The nature of the injustice that black Americans face is, in part, the inability to mitigate through their own actions the aggressive behavior of police officers. Racial profiling and bias in law enforcement (whether conscious or unconscious), segregation, and the concentration of black people in higher-crime urban neighborhoods result in far more, and more dangerous, interactions with police for blacks than whites.[26] And black people are aware that behaving the same as whites may, for them, result in violent or even deadly confrontations. Freddie Gray was apprehended after he made eye contact with and then ran away from officers.[27] Michael Brown was jaywalking when he was stopped. In other words, compared to whites, blacks' interactions with police are frequent and risky and so, police presence for many black people is marked by anxiety, fear, and mistrust.[28]

For police to be tolerated, or even welcomed, as a benign, ordering element at protests against police brutality, especially where the majority of the demonstrators are black, sends a contradictory message about a central aspect of this injustice. It communicates that officers' actions are potentially predictable, provided black civilians' behavior is not such that use-of-force is warranted. But, as such protests are at pains to communicate to a white majority for whom this is the norm, this is not the case. Rather, attempts by black people to obey orders, run, or verbally challenge—in short, attempts to behave in precisely the ways that whites do under the same circumstances—are more likely to have deleterious effects.

Witnessing the Baltimore and Ferguson protesters, we were struck by the communicative potential of some of their actions: Think of the teenagers in Baltimore, penned in at Mondawmin Mall, hurling bottles and rocks toward police dressed in riot gear. Recall Edward Crawford in his American flag T-shirt, throwing a burning tear gas canister back toward officers deployed to quell the unrest in Ferguson.[29] Though perhaps not intended to communicate a message, these acts of violent lawbreaking nevertheless evoked a sense of a community using the meager means available to ward off the advances of a powerful, militaristic force. They positioned the demonstrators as members of communities under siege. Given that the injustice at issue crucially concerns the unchecked power of the police deployed against an oppressed minority, it is possible that the only way to consistently communicate this message is via violent protest. In contrast to protests where the police are accepted as neutral, or even benign, staging protests in which black demonstrators challenge police presence by warding off militaristic-looking police with bottles and rocks, or use the police's own tools of dispersal against them, could communicate that the arbitrary interference of law enforcement in the lives of black Americans is central to the injustice in question.[30] It consistently conveys the message that law enforcement is a threat to black protesters and black communities because their actions are unpredictable and, potentially, unrestrained.

This is true even if the police respond to protests in a controlled manner. Although police might treat protests as a special case, nevertheless nonviolent protests of police brutality could interfere with communicating about the injustice at issue. For one, the intended audience may not notice the differences between protests (e.g., media attention and political pressure) and ordinary, everyday interactions between police and black civilians. Or, they may be disinclined to attribute the nonviolent outcome of the protests to these special circumstances, rather than to the behavior of the protesters. This could inadvertently bolster the mistaken notion that blacks could avoid being killed were they simply more cooperative with the police.

Moreover, the use of nonviolence in protests, where police behavior is sometimes (though not reliably) predictable, ignores the fact that law enforcement's arbitrary interference in the lives of black people is sanctioned by laws and policies, both formal and informal, and routinely upheld in the courts. Permissive police department policies allow officers wide latitude in their choice of tactics, while the Supreme Court's "objective reasonableness" standard establishes a high legal bar for determining excessive force. Under the guise of "police discretion," racial profiling and the (conscious or unconscious) biases of individual officers are protected and institutionalized. Meanwhile, standard mechanisms of oversight and redress, such as media attention (including viral videos captured on police cameras or civilian cell phones), judicial proceedings, and legal changes have proven insufficient to curb this injustice in the ordinary case.[31] Thus, civilians' inability to mitigate police violence and brutality also obtains at the institutional level. This both underscores the need for protest and highlights the threat that police pose, individually and collectively. Without substantial changes to law enforcement institutions, police brutality against black people will continue.

However, that the audience to whom the protesters are speaking may be inclined to notice some features of the protests while ignoring others raises a further worry: doesn't violence carry a greater chance of being misunderstood? Violence might avoid inconsistency in the protesters' message, but it could also overshadow that message, such that it will still be the case that in every instance, nonviolent protest would be preferable.[32] Imagine that instead of throwing bottles and bricks, demonstrators used white protesters to shield black protesters from police. This strategy was deployed in South African demonstrations against tuition hikes where, at the request of black protest leaders, white students surrounded black student protesters in an effort to protect them from police violence.[33] A similar strategy used to communicative, rather than pragmatic, effect might also send the message that law enforcement, as an institution, unfairly targets blacks.

The mere fact that we can imagine other nonviolent communicative strategies does not rule out sometimes needing to use controlled, nonlethal violence to communicate. Perhaps there will be cases where black protesters cannot depend on white allies to help carry the message. The success of some nonviolent communicative strategies depends on a sufficient number of willing whites and a good working relationship between black and white protesters. This relationship may be hard to come by. For example, protesters have accused white anarchists of co-opting BLM protests to promote their broader anti-policing agenda. Also, whites have expressed anger or frustration when BLM chapters designate certain events as "blacks-only spaces." These are the sorts of tensions common to liberal societies with oppressed minorities who are fighting for justice,[34] and so it is an open question whether such nonviolent communicative strategies are even pragmatically available to protesters.

More broadly, everything from the demographics of the protesters to their imaginative capacities are background constraints on the communicative resources available. Nonviolence may be communicatively preferable, but sometimes violent protest may be the only means of consistent communication. But whether communicative violence is morally or pragmatically justified is a further question. That only one strategy for communication of a particular message is open does not necessarily give the oppressed group license to employ that strategy. They may be required to wait until a shift in resources means that a different communicative strategy becomes available. With that in mind, we move to a discussion of the moral and pragmatic considerations that might still rule out communicatively required violent protest.

MORAL CONSIDERATIONS

We now turn our focus to moral arguments against interpersonal violent protest (throwing bottles and bricks at police, etc.).[35] Moral arguments that would categorically rule out such violence—even when it is communicatively required—might include the following: (1) with the use of violence protesters are unfairly targeting police who are not actually responsible for the injustice in question, (2) the protesters are failing to respect police by treating them as mere means to the protesters' ends, and (3) violent protesters are unfairly placing nonviolent protesters and communities at risk, both by their own hands and at the hands of the police. In addition, they may subject all members of black communities to greater risk by further straining the relationship between police and black civilians. We examine each argument in turn.

Certain acts of interpersonal violence during protests, such as targeting innocent bystanders and their private property, are morally impermissible. Only when individuals have forfeited their rights to safety, security, and property, either through consent or, more commonly, through responsibility for the injustice at issue, do they become liable to attack.[36] Innocent bystanders, by definition, are not responsible for any wrongdoing, and so are not liable to be attacked, even by people acting in their own defense.[37] It is not clear that police officers like those attacked during Baltimore and Ferguson are innocent in the (morally) relevant sense. For their targeting to be unfair, it would have to be the case that they are not responsible for the injustice at issue; but this claim strikes us as suspect. It seems likely that certain acts of violence, while perhaps not morally acceptable against ordinary civilians, may be morally permissible against police.

When police officers, dressed in militaristic garb, advance on black communities with the express purpose of "quelling unrest," it is appropriate for protesters to view those officers as, if not fully liable for the unjust threat they pose, at the very least as posing an unjust threat over which they have some control. This is especially true given that these encroachments are likely to involve (still more) risky and unpredictable interactions with police, which black people know threaten their well-being, safety, and security. The police are reasonably read as posing an immediate unjust threat, and as possibly liable for that threat, because they are in the midst of acting on behalf of an institution that threatens the bodily integrity of black civilians. And this is so regardless of whether the individual officers who are directly acting to further that injustice agree with, or are even conscious of, law enforcement's unjust treatment of black people.

This permits protesters wide latitude in interpreting officers' actions as unjustly threatening. In general, protesters need not assume officers' peaceful intentions, nor take it for granted that officers are likely to either prioritize protesters' safety over other considerations, or protect protesters from violent attacks (either by counter-protesters or their fellow officers). As such, protesters have more moral leeway in how they respond to officers. For example, they may ignore orders to disperse, even when those orders are couched in terms of community safety or security, and they may react violently, throwing bottles and bricks to ward off officers or break through barriers.[38] Such defensive maneuvers are morally permissible, given the well-known unjust threat that acting officers pose. While the primary ground for violent protest is its communicative necessity, when the police's relationship to the injustice at issue is such that it is reasonable to read their actions as posing an immediate unjust threat, violence may also be morally permitted.[39]

This only permits violent protest against those police officers who are reasonably interpreted as being in the midst of posing an immediate and/or serious unjust threat. Consider the sniper who killed white police officers at random in Dallas in response to police brutality.[40] Killing random police officers, who aren't currently advancing on black communities, is outside the boundaries of protest. The Dallas sniper's actions send exactly the wrong message about the nature of the injustice. They indicate that individual police officers are the problem, when what is primarily at issue is a political institution that fails to regulate its agents and even encourages them to act in unjust ways. More generally, lethal violence forecloses the possibility of political communication in a way that nonlethal violence does not. One cannot communicate with fellow community members, even those who are perpetrating or enabling injustices, when they are dead.[41]

Noticing the distinction between this attack and the protests in Baltimore and Ferguson helps to address the second moral complaint against violent protest: that protesters fail to respect police by treating them as mere means to the protesters' communicative ends. But, violence may be precisely what is required to treat those officers as ends in themselves. As Robert Holmes argues, the imperfect circumstances of our lives sometimes make it the case that the only way to respect others as ends in themselves is to hold them responsible for the injustices that they do. This is not punishment, but a way of reminding them that they can, and must, do better.[42] Ideally, holding them responsible will take a nonviolent form, but in some cases, Holmes admits, limited violence may be morally justified, if not required.[43] For protesters to engage in nonlethal violence against police officers, then, might be the opposite of treating those officers as mere means; doing so can actually respect them as agents by holding them responsible, via treating them as individuals capable of acting with discretion.[44]

This takes us to the final worry, that violent protesters unfairly place nonviolent protesters and communities at risk, both by their own hands and at the hands of the police. This concern highlights that the use of violence ought to be constrained in many of the ways we have already argued. When would-be violent protesters cannot aim at morally appropriate targets, they may not engage in violence, regardless of whether it is communicatively required to send their message. Protesters must be mindful of the communicative context in which they're operating, the vulnerabilities of their and other communities, and the potential for violence to spill over into civilian spaces. Protesters must account for and mitigate these risks.[45]

The second but related issue is that using violent protest runs the real risk of provoking retaliation by the police.[46] First, it is important to note that all protest against police brutality, violent or not, runs the risk of provoking retaliation. Also, risk assessments, and determinations of how much risk is morally acceptable, are complicated, and are best left to those who are most likely to be subject to the risks in question.[47] It is not up to us to either assess the risks involved or determine how much risk is morally acceptable; these assessments and determinations are, in the first instance, for the protesters, the members of communities where such protests occur, and those who are victims of the relevant injustice. On the one hand, the police could retaliate and that could be dangerous, if not lethal. But, on the other hand, it is already dangerous to be black, precisely because of police brutality. If violent protests can help solve this problem, then the risks may be worth the reward. The risk is morally significant, to be sure; but given the situation of existent police brutality, it does not clearly tell against engaging in violent protest against police brutality. Arriving at stronger conclusions than this about the moral acceptability of taking such risks depends upon determining the value of trying to eradicate police brutality, and that is primarily (although not exclusively) a question for those put at risk.[48]

Additionally, police have options in how they respond to violent protest. They can choose to retaliate against nonviolent protesters, communities, and black people more generally, or they can engage in de-escalation tactics both during and after protests. Such non-retaliatory options (that follow the community policing model[49]) might go some way toward solving the injustice being protested. That police do not engage in such de-escalation strategies is their moral error, not the protesters'. To claim otherwise is to blame the victim; it is to say that the protesters "made" the police retaliate, that police cannot help but lash out against those who (rightfully) point out deep injustices in their practices, policies, and behaviors. The morality of the protesters' choice to engage in communicatively required violent protest should not be determined by how the police choose to respond.[50]

PRAGMATIC CONSIDERATIONS

All protest is subject to pragmatic considerations: when it is clear to the oppressed group that violence will be ineffective, they should refrain from engaging in it. But, the effectiveness of any particular protest can take different forms, and cannot be judged by immediate public or private response. The Occupy Movement was widely derided as a failure in the months following Occupy's main series of protests.[51] Since then, some social movement theorists have credited it with kickstarting an international conversation on economic inequality.[52] Those quick to naysay particular acts of protest as ineffective frequently consider only short-term effectiveness. Protest is about the long game though, and large-scale sociopolitical changes often have many partial causes, rather than a singular cause. No one protest, march, speech, free breakfast, legal challenge, strike, or bus ride led directly to the Civil Rights Act of 1968. Suitably morally constrained violent protest may be initially ineffective, but to the extent that it can cut through the "noise" and attract media and political attention to its message, it can be effective in the longer run.[53]

One might argue that violent protest is always ineffective compared to nonviolent protest. According to Erica Chenoweth and Maria J. Stephan's study of past civil resistance movements, nonviolent movements are twice as likely to successfully achieve their goals as violent movements.[54] Thus, they advocate for a strictly nonviolent approach to civil disobedience and protest on pragmatic grounds. This seems too definite, given both that they admit that violent movements sometimes successfully achieve their goals, and that their quantitative analysis defines violence narrowly, as armed insurgencies, while their qualitative analysis defines violence broadly, as not only armed insurrection but also throwing stones, bottles, bricks and other improvised weapons, and fists. This mismatch suggests that they are drawing an inappropriately strong conclusion from the available quantitative data about the relationship between strict nonviolence and success.[55]

Moreover, their categorization of "violent" versus "nonviolent" movements raises the further difficulty of determining which actions count as part of a movement and which do not. Though popular liberal imagination often treats the protesting party as a monolith, in practice, this is never the case. Rather, multiple protesting groups work, sometimes independently and sometimes in tandem, to end unjust practices, laws, and policies, using various strategies and tactics.[56] Many paradigmatic nonviolent movements, including those ostensibly led by Gandhi, King, and Mandela, also contained or coexisted alongside violent elements, which were arguably crucial to the overall movement's success.

Take the civil rights movement in the United States. Though King and his nonviolent civil disobedience movement are now commemorated as paragons of peaceful protest, Malcolm X, along with the Nation of Islam (and later the Black Panthers and the more radicalized iteration of the Student Nonviolent Coordinating Committee), provided an alternative for the many black Americans who were unimpressed with King's message of nonviolent resistance.[57] As Malcolm X put it in his famous "The Ballot or the Bullet" speech, "There's new strategy coming in. It'll be Molotov cocktails this month, hand grenades next month, and something else next month. It'll be ballots, or it'll be bullets. It'll be liberty, or it will be death."[58] In addition, a long tradition of black Southerners engaging in armed self-defense, as well as several armed confrontations with the KKK in the early 1960s, may be part of the confluence of factors that pushed the government toward negotiation with the nonviolent wing of the Civil Rights Movement by the mid-1960s.[59] These violent and nonviolent factions, though in tension with each other, worked alongside one another on a practical level.[60]

Juliet Hooker argues that the typical, sanitized view of black protesters during the civil rights era, as people who used peaceful protest to great effect, depends on a misunderstanding of how white audiences read those protests. On that idealized view, she writes,

> Peaceful acquiescence to racial terror is viewed as an exemplary act of citizenship due to the assumed capacity of this act of democratic sacrifice

to sway the moral orientations of members of the dominant racial group who, upon observing such naked displays of violence, are shamed into renouncing racial injustice.[61]

Supposedly, it is through the contradiction between white violence (i.e., police beating protesters) and black acquiescence (i.e., protesters remaining peaceful in the face of such beatings) that white audiences to these displays are forced to make a choice to either embrace the white violence or disavow it. But as Hooker notes, citing Hannah Arendt's "Reflections on Little Rock," a wholly different reaction is possible.

Arendt criticizes black efforts at school desegregation as motivated by self-interest—the desire of black Americans for upward social mobility rather than legal rights. She empathizes with white Southerners who claim the right to decide how and in whose company their children should be socialized. Hooker draws from this reaction that rather than causing shame, such protests can and do induce resentment—blacks are seen as needlessly riling up tensions—and defensiveness. However, it is the narrative that black protesters convinced a white audience to support their cause through peaceful acquiescence which dominates the popular imagination about the civil rights era.[62] This narrative is trotted out to critique more radical forms of black politics, including the use of violence.

The historical record is more complicated than people recognize: the lesson "nonviolence just works better" cannot be straightforwardly drawn from the history of protest. As Hooker notes, current responses to BLM present similar worries for the potential of peaceful acquiescence to transform its white audience through shame in this way. Insulated from interaction with other racial groups through racial segregation and fed a steady diet of sanitized historical narratives toward racial progress, many whites assume that the United States has entered a post-racial era, or at the least see the problems of racial injustice as located in some other part of the country. Given this, defensiveness and resentment are more likely responses than shame. Peaceful acquiescence may not work; violent protest may be needed to make communicative progress.

We conclude that violent protest is not strictly ruled out on pragmatic grounds. Once protesters have determined that an act of violent protest is required to communicate a message, they must also weigh the pragmatic pros and cons. For instance, the violence of the Baltimore protests—perhaps predictably—led to the Governor declaring a state of emergency and calling in the National Guard. One might say this was a bad result, pragmatically speaking, because it increased the presence of security forces in Baltimore. But drawing out such a governmental response could be pragmatically effective if it helps highlight the daily state of emergency of many black American communities.

NOTES

1. This chapter was originally published as Jennifer Kling and Megan Mitchell, "Bottles and Bricks: Rethinking the Prohibition Against Violent Protest," *Radical Philosophy Review* 22, no. 2 (2019), 209–37. doi:10.5840/radphilrev20197997. Our thanks to the journal for permission to republish it with alterations here.

2. Sheryl Gay Stolberg and Stephen Babcock, "Scenes of Chaos in Baltimore as Thousands Protest Freddie Gray's Death," *New York Times*, April 25, 2015.

3. Eric Bradner, "Obama: 'No Excuse' for Violence in Baltimore," *CNN*, April 28, 2015.

4. John Rawls, *A Theory of Justice, Revised Edition* (Cambridge, MA: Belknap Press, 1999), 319–23. See also Candice Delmas, "Civil Disobedience," *Philosophical Compass* 11, no. 11 (2016), 682–83.

5. There are serious disputes over what counts as violence. The sorts of actions that we defend in this chapter include throwing rocks, bricks, and other debris at police officers. Though dressed in riot gear, police in Baltimore sustained injuries up to and including broken bones and being knocked unconscious. While we assume it here, in chapter 3, we argue for a conception of violence that includes these actions.

6. Kimberley Brownlee raises this possibility. Kimberley Brownlee, *Conscience and Conviction: The Case for Civil Disobedience* (Oxford: Oxford University Press, 2012), 20.

7. For more on how we view contemporary liberal societies and their injustices, see chapter 1.

8. Kimberley Brownlee, "Features of a Paradigm Case of Civil Disobedience," *Res Publica* 10, no. 4 (2004), 349–50; Brownlee, *Conscience and Conviction: The Case for Civil Disobedience*, 21–24; Delmas, "Civil Disobedience," 683–84; Candice Delmas, *A Duty to Resist: When Disobedience should be Uncivil* (New York, NY: Oxford University Press, 2018), 58–62. See also John Morreall, "The Justifiability of Violent Civil Disobedience," *Canadian Journal of Philosophy* 6, no. 1 (1976), 35–47; Piero Moraro, "Violent Civil Disobedience and Willingness to Accept Punishment," *Essays in Philosophy* 8,

no. 2 (2007), 1–15; A. John Simmons, "Disobedience and its Objects," *Boston University Law Review* 90, no. 4 (2010), 1805–31.

9. We develop an account of the unique communicative functions of violence throughout the book.

10. This sets the stage for a longer discussion of these issues in chapters 4, 5, and 6.

11. Edward Crawford, for instance, claimed to have thrown a tear gas canister not toward police, but away from children. Mary Emily O'Hara, "Ferguson Protester Edward Crawford, Subject of Iconic Photo, found Dead," *NBC News,* May 5, 2017.

12. Rawls, *A Theory of Justice, Revised Edition,* 321.

13. Brownlee, "Features of a Paradigm Case of Civil Disobedience," 349–50.

14. Rawls, *A Theory of Justice, Revised Edition,* 364–67.

15. Brownlee, *Conscience and Conviction: The Case for Civil Disobedience,* 21–22.

16. Other examples of nonviolent protest that are forceful and threatening, if not coercive, include economic boycotts and coordinated DDOS attacks on automated infrastructure systems.

17. As Simmons writes, "it is not evident why an act of violence must always fail the test of counting as an appropriately political act, by necessarily expressing contempt or diminished respect for law and politics—especially if the violent act is carefully presented to the public as protest, if it is isolated (an unusual act in an otherwise nonviolent life), if it has been preceded by passive political efforts, and if it is followed by non-evasion and acceptance of punishment." Simmons, "Disobedience and its Objects," 1808.

18. Rawls, *A Theory of Justice, Revised Edition,* 336.

19. It might seem that in allowing herself to be arrested, the messages of fidelity to law and the desire to remain in the community are transferred from the nature of the lawbreaking to the act of submitting to arrest. And the two are tightly tied together in the concept of justified lawbreaking protest because in general (and certainly in Rawls' nearly just society) those who perform nonviolent civil disobedience can (and Rawls thinks, must) allow themselves to be arrested. But both committing a violent act and then attempting to avoid arrest (by, for example, running away) may be essential to the message in some acts of protest. How, in those cases, can the actors communicate fidelity to law through their actions? One thought is that they may not be able to, at least within the protest act itself. In these cases, they can try to communicate that message directly by, for instance, issuing a statement explaining their actions. How effective that method will be (as opposed to engaging in nonviolence and submitting to arrest) is likely to vary by context. Regardless, it doesn't appear that nonviolence is conceptually required to transmit this message. Even in

cases of nonviolent direct action, there will likely be parts of the message that have to be communicated directly, as the full intention behind the message is rarely available from the act alone.

20. From Matt Vasilogambros, "Did Colin Kaepernick's Protest Fail?" *The Atlantic,* August 30, 2016: "Critics have called his actions unpatriotic and disrespectful. Donald Trump . . . even chimed in, saying Kaepernick 'should find a country that works better for him.'"

21. Brownlee, "Features of a Paradigm Case of Civil Disobedience," 337.

22. Brownlee, *Conscience and Conviction: The Case for Civil Disobedience,* 24.

23. Andrew Cohen, "The Black Students Who Wouldn't Leave the Lunch Counter," *The Atlantic*, January 10, 2014; Michael Walzer, "The Young: A Cup of Coffee and a Seat," *Dissent*, 1960.

24. Christopher W. Schmidt, *The Sit-Ins: Protest and Legal Change in the Civil Rights Era* (Chicago: University of Chicago Press, 2018), 5–11, and chapter 2.

25. For evidence of this as the accepted norm, see the criticism Charlottesville police received after a 2017 Unite the Right rally left one counterprotester dead and many injured. Timothy Heaphy, "Independent Review of the 2017 Protest Events in Charlottesville, Virginia" (Washington, DC: Hunton & Williams, 2018), 159–62.

26. Black Americans are subject to more frequent police interactions than whites. In a recent study of traffic stops from twenty U.S. states over six year, blacks were more likely than whites to be stopped, ticketed, searched, and arrested. Emma Pierson et al., "A Large Scale Analysis of Racial Disparities in Police Stops Across the United States," *Stanford Open Policing Project Working Paper* (2017), 4–7. Researchers did not claim these stops are caused by racial bias, although they did cite race as a relevant factor in the officer's decision to search (11). Studies from particular localities (Ferguson, New York, and Boston) suggest that race is directly relevant to officers' decisions to initiate a traffic or pedestrian stop. Nazgol Ghandnoosh, "Black Lives Matter: Eliminating Racial Inequity in the Criminal Justice System," *The Sentencing Project* (2015), 10. Meanwhile, with regard to the encounters themselves, a 2016 study found race to be a relevant factor in officers' use of nonlethal force, which includes tactics like being pushed to the ground, handcuffed, or pepper sprayed. Interestingly, the same study found no evidence of antiblack discrimination in officers' use of lethal force. Roland G. Fryer Jr, "An Empirical Analysis of Racial Differences in Police use of Force," *NBER Working Papers 22399* (January 2018), 14–15, 26. However, as the author notes, the study did not examine whether racial bias motivated initial police-civilian contact, nor does it rule out racial bias as a relevant factor in any particular case (27). Compared to nonlethal use of force, use of lethal force is relatively rare.

27. One might argue that running from officers, as Freddie Gray, Walter Scott, and Antwon Rose did before they were shot or killed, caused the confrontation. But, given the data on use-of-force cited above, it's clear that cooperating with the officers' demands could have resulted in injury. Moreover, in Gray's case, the officers charged with his murder claimed his injuries were sustained while in custody. Although their account is highly suspect, taking these officers at their word could make running an even more appealing strategy for black Americans, since surviving the initial encounter with police is only one phase of a potentially multistep process, each part of which renders them vulnerable to use-of-force. Even if the officers' actions were a response to Gray's attempted evasion, the mere fact that officers responded with such callousness toward someone in their custody could make it reasonable to attempt, if possible, to avoid them. In any case, waiting passively for police to decide whether to search one's person is an indignity that anyone could have good reason to avoid.

28. A meta-analysis of ninety-two studies found that blacks tend to have more negative perceptions and attitudes toward police than either whites or Hispanics. Jennifer H. Peck, "Minority Perceptions of Police: A State-of-Art-Review," *Policing: An International Journal on Police Strategies and Management* 38, no. 1 (2015), 74.

29. Robert Cohen, "Untitled Photo of Ferguson Protests," *St. Louis Post-Dispatch*, August 13, 2014.

30. Importantly, this analysis need not be constrained only to the case of contemporary police brutality against black Americans, but may also be extended to other cases where security forces deploy unchecked power against oppressed minorities (situations in Palestine and Myanmar at the time of writing—2020—may be of this kind). However, extending this analysis requires, at the least, that the society in question either is, or is perceived as, liberal, that the unchecked power of the security force(s) is of the sort we describe and is consistently deployed, that the minority is oppressed in the ways we describe, and that the communicatively required violent protests do not contravene moral or pragmatic limits.

31. Derek Chauvin's 2021 conviction for the murder of George Floyd is the exception that proves the rule.

32. It is impossible to guarantee that a message will not be misunderstood (consider the Colin Kaepernick case discussed above). Norms of political communication do not require that an act, to be communicatively justified, be incapable of misinterpretation. So, the question is about the likelihood of misinterpretation, and thus about what is preferable for effective communication.

33. Lucy Sherriff, "White Students Form a Human Shield to Protect Black #FeesMustFall Protesters from South African Police," *HuffPost UK*, Oct 22, 2015.

34. For more on the features of nonideal liberal societies, see chapter 1.

35. This discussion is not a full moral defense of all kinds of violent protest, nor, for reasons articulated earlier, the particular incidents that occurred in Baltimore and Ferguson. Rather, the following arguments are a starting point for such analysis. We continue this analysis in the subsequent chapters.

36. It is an open question whether there are any innocent bystanders in liberal societies marked by oppression. We discuss responsibility for injustice at length in chapter 5.

37. Called the innocent bystander exception in the self-defense literature, this moral principle is defended by, among others, Judith Jarvis Thomson, "Self-Defense," *Philosophy & Public Affairs* 20, no. 4 (1991), 298; Thomas Nagel, "War and Massacre," *Philosophy & Public Affairs* 1, no. 2 (1972), 130–32; Jeff McMahan, *Killing in War* (Oxford: Oxford University Press, 2009), 110–15.

38. Precisely how violent protesters are morally permitted to be in such cases, while respecting the nonlethality constraint, is a difficult question. Perhaps protesters may not aim directly at officers or, if they are permitted to aim, they must aim toward parts of the officer that are heavily fortified, like shields, and avoid heads or other vulnerable areas. For more discussion of the constraints on protesters, see chapters 4 and 6.

39. We discuss this argument in more depth in chapter 5.

40. Manny Fernandez, Richard Pérez-Peña, and Jonah Engel Bromwich, "Five Dallas Officers were Killed as Payback, Police Chief Says," *New York Times*, July 8, 2016.

41. If the immediate threat posed to protesters is lethal, then they might be justified in responding with lethal force themselves; however, that could take them out of the realm of protest and into the realm of revolution. When you begin killing your political opponents, rather than trying to persuade them to change, it is a good sign that you are more revolutionary than protester. For more on this, see chapter 7.

42. Robert Holmes, *The Ethics of Nonviolence: Essays by Robert L. Holmes* (New York: Bloomsbury, 2013), 157–74.

43. Holmes, *The Ethics of Nonviolence: Essays by Robert L. Holmes*, 158. Holmes admits that absolute pacifism is "clearly untenable," because of facts about our current sociopolitical situations (158). Still, the general need to respect others (and ourselves) as ends constrains what violence we may do; we must strive, as a way of living, toward the creation of a nonviolent world (157–74). This is exactly what the violent protest under discussion is trying to do: at its best, it sends a message about the nature of police brutality toward black civilians, in hopes that understanding it might lead to its cessation. The achievement of a nonviolent world may thus require some suitably constrained violent protest.

44. As Onora O'Neill argues, we best treat people as ends in themselves, rather than as mere means, when we treat them as individuals with their own ends. This is why the claim that police "were just doing their jobs" does not excuse their actions. When individuals take on role responsibilities, they *add* those responsibilities to what is already required of them as private individuals; so, respecting them requires holding them responsible as individuals for what they do in both their public and private lives. Onora O'Neill, "The Moral Perplexities of Famine Relief," in *Matters of Life and Death*, eds. Tom L. Beauchamp and Tom Regan (Philadelphia: Temple University Press, 1980), 260–98.

45. We discuss the responsibilities of protesters in more depth in chapter 6.

46. Richard A. Oppel Jr., "West Baltimore's Police Presence Drops, and Murders Soar," *New York Times*, June 12, 2015.

47. Tim Lewens, "Introduction," in *Risk: Philosophical Perspectives*, ed. Tim Lewens (New York: Routledge, 2007), 1–20.

48. Sven Ove Hansson, "Risk and Ethics: Three Approaches," in *Risk: Philosophical Perspectives*, ed. Tim Lewens (New York: Routledge, 2007), 21–35.

49. Gary W. Cordner, "Elements of Community Policing," in *Policing Perspectives: An Anthology*, eds. Gary W. Cordner and Larry K. Gaines (Oxford: Oxford University Press, 1998), 137–49.

50. What the police might, or are likely to, do can affect the pragmatics of protesters' decisions, but not the morality of them. For further discussion of these issues, see chapter 5.

51. Andy Ostroy, "The Failure of Occupy Wall Street," *Huffington Post*, May 31, 2012; Micah White, "Occupy and Black Lives Matter Failed. We can either Win Wars or Win Elections," *The Guardian*, August 28, 2017.

52. Aaron Taube, "Maybe Occupy Wall Street Wasn't such a Failure After All," *Business Insider*, September 17, 2013; Michael Levitin, "The Triumph of Occupy Wall Street," *The Atlantic*, June 10, 2015.

53. Gene Demby, "The Butterfly Effects of Ferguson," *NPR*, August 11, 2016.

54. Violent movements succeed in achieving their goals 26 percent of the time, while nonviolent movements have a 53 percent chance of success. Erica Chenoweth and Maria J. Stephan, *Why Civil Resistance Works: The Strategic Logic of Nonviolent Conflict* (New York: Columbia University Press, 2011), 7–11.

55. Mohammad Ali Kadivar and Neil Ketchley, "Sticks, Stones, and Molotov Cocktails: Unarmed Collective Violence and Democratization," *Socius: Sociological Research for a Dynamic World* 4 (2018), 1–16.

56. These groups may not align themselves politically with each other; nevertheless, they are aligned both in the minds of the oppressors and by the

oppressive circumstances that they share. In discussing this research, Delmas makes a similar point, noting that "most of the civil resistance movements they classify as nonviolent, from the anti-apartheid struggle in South Africa to the First Palestinian Intifada, often in fact include violent flanks." Delmas, *A Duty to Resist: When Disobedience should be Uncivil*, 58.

57. Joshua Bloom and Waldo E. Martin, *Black Against Empire: The History and Politics of the Black Panther Party* (California: University of California Press, 2012), 3. See also the 1963 television program "The Negro and the American Promise," wherein James Baldwin states that "the Black Muslim movement is the only one in the country we can call grassroots . . . Malcolm articulates for Negroes, their suffering . . . he corroborates their reality." *The Negro and the American Promise,* Television (Boston, MA: WGBH, 1963).

58. Malcolm X, "The Ballot or the Bullet," in *The Radical Reader*, eds. Timothy Patrick McCarthy and John McMillian (New York: The New Press, 2003), 386.

59. Akinyele Umoja, *We Will Shoot Back: Armed Resistance in the Mississippi Freedom Movement* (New York: New York University Press, 2013), 126; "The Time has Come," *Eyes on the Prize: America's Civil Rights Movement 1954-1985,* Television, directed by Henry Hampton (PBS, 1990).

60. A fact that King clearly recognized in his "Letter from Birmingham Jail," in which he casts support of his movement as the only alternative to a violent black nationalism. Delmas also calls attention to this, arguing that a sanitized historical narrative of the civil rights movement acts as an obscurant, limiting the opportunities of protesters for emancipatory political action in the face of continuing antiblack racism. Delmas, *A Duty to Resist: When Disobedience should be Uncivil*, 29–35.

61. Juliet Hooker, "Black Lives Matter and the Paradoxes of U.S. Black Politics: From Democratic Sacrifice to Democratic Repair," *Political Theory* 44, no. 4 (2016), 458.

62. Hooker attributes such readings to an impoverished account of white psychology that fails to account for the epistemic defects that are part and parcel of being a privileged group in a society with racial oppression. This complements our analysis of contemporary liberal societies in chapter 1. Hooker, "Black Lives Matter and the Paradoxes of U.S. Black Politics: From Democratic Sacrifice to Democratic Repair," 452–55.

BIBLIOGRAPHY

Bloom, Joshua and Waldo E. Martin. *Black Against Empire: The History and Politics of the Black Panther Party*. California: University of California Press, 2012.

Bradner, Eric. "Obama: 'No Excuse' for Violence in Baltimore." *CNN,* April 28, 2015. https://www.cnn.com/2015/04/28/politics/obama-baltimore-viol ent-protests/index.html.

Brownlee, Kimberley. *Conscience and Conviction: The Case for Civil Disobedience.* Oxford: Oxford University Press, 2012.

———. "Features of a Paradigm Case of Civil Disobedience." *Res Publica* 10, no. 4 (2004): 337–351.

Chenoweth, Erica and Maria J. Stephan. *Why Civil Resistance Works: The Strategic Logic of Nonviolent Conflict.* New York: Columbia University Press, 2011.

Cohen, Andrew. "The Black Students Who Wouldn't Leave the Lunch Counter." *The Atlantic,* January 10, 2014. https://www.theatlantic.com/ national/archive/2014/01/the-black-students-who-wouldnt-leave-the-lunch-counter/282986/.

Cohen, Robert. "Untitled Photo of Ferguson Protests." *St. Louis Post-Dispatch,* August 13, 2014. https://www.stltoday.com/news/local/metro/the-pulitzer-prize-winning-photographs-from-the-post-dispatch/collection_7a5793c3-9 a55-534c-b84a-a27d6d08ef5f.html.

Cordner, Gary W. "Elements of Community Policing." In *Policing Perspectives: An Anthology*, edited by Cordner, Gary W. and Larry K. Gaines, 137–149. Oxford: Oxford University Press, 1998.

Delmas, Candice. "Civil Disobedience." *Philosophical Compass* 11, no. 11 (2016): 681–691.

———. *A Duty to Resist: When Disobedience should be Uncivil.* New York, NY: Oxford University Press, 2018.

Demby, Gene. "The Butterfly Effects of Ferguson." *NPR,* August 11, 2016. https://www.npr.org/sections/codeswitch/2016/08/11/489494015/the-butte rfly-effects-of-ferguson.

Fernandez, Manny, Richard Pérez-Peña, and Jonah Engel Bromwich. "Five Dallas Officers were Killed as Payback, Police Chief Says." *New York Times,* July 8, 2016. https://www.nytimes.com/2016/07/09/us/dallas-police -shooting.html.

Fryer, Roland G., Jr. "An Empirical Analysis of Racial Differences in Police use of Force." *NBER Working Papers 22399* (January 2018).

Ghandnoosh, Nazgol. "Black Lives Matter: Eliminating Racial Inequity in the Criminal Justice System." *The Sentencing Project* (2015). https://sentenc ingproject.org/wp-content/uploads/2015/11/Black-Lives-Matter.pdf.

Hansson, Sven Ove. "Risk and Ethics: Three Approaches." In *Risk: Philosophical Perspectives*, edited by Tim Lewens, 21–35. New York: Routledge, 2007.

Heaphy, Timothy. "Independent Review of the 2017 Protest Events in Charlottesville, Virginia." (Washington, DC: Hunton & Williams, 2018). https

://www.huntonak.com/images/content/3/4/v4/34613/final-report-ada-compl
iant-ready.pdf.

Holmes, Robert. *The Ethics of Nonviolence: Essays by Robert L. Holmes*. New
York: Bloomsbury, 2013.

Hooker, Juliet. "Black Lives Matter and the Paradoxes of U.S. Black Politics:
From Democratic Sacrifice to Democratic Repair." *Political Theory* 44, no.
4 (2016): 448–469.

Kadivar, Mohammad Ali and Neil Ketchley. "Sticks, Stones, and Molotov
Cocktails: Unarmed Collective Violence and Democratization." *Socius:
Sociological Research for a Dynamic World* 4 (2018): 1–16.

Kling, Jennifer and Megan Mitchell. "Bottles and Bricks: Rethinking the
Prohibition Against Violent Protest." *Radical Philosophy Review* 22, no. 2
(2019): 209–237.

Levitin, Michael. "The Triumph of Occupy Wall Street." *The Atlantic,* June 10,
2015. https://www.theatlantic.com/politics/archive/2015/06/the-triumph-of
-occupy-wall-street/395408/.

Lewens, Tim. "Introduction." In *Risk: Philosophical Perspectives*, edited by
Lewens, Tim, 1-20. New York: Routledge, 2007.

Malcolm X. "The Ballot or the Bullet." In *The Radical Reader*, edited by
McCarthy, Timothy Patrick and John McMillian, 382–389. New York: The
New Press, 2003.

McMahan, Jeff. *Killing in War*. Oxford: Oxford University Press, 2009.

Moraro, Piero. "Violent Civil Disobedience and Willingness to Accept Punishment." *Essays in Philosophy* 8, no. 2 (2007): 1–15.

Morreall, John. "The Justifiability of Violent Civil Disobedience." *Canadian
Journal of Philosophy* 6, no. 1 (1976): 35–47.

Nagel, Thomas. "War and Massacre." *Philosophy & Public Affairs* 1, no. 2
(1972): 123–144.

O'Neill, Onora. "The Moral Perplexities of Famine Relief." In *Matters of Life
and Death*, edited by Beauchamp, Tom L. and Tom Regan, 260–298. Philadelphia: Temple University Press, 1980.

O'Hara, Mary Emily. "Ferguson Protester Edward Crawford, Subject of Iconic
Photo, foundDead." *NBC News,* May 5, 2017. https://www.nbcnews.com/
news/us-news/ferguson-protester-edward-crawford-subject-iconic-photo-fo
und-dead-n755401.

Oppel Jr., Richard A. "West Baltimore's Police Presence Drops, and Murders
Soar." *New York Times,* June 12, 2015. https://www.nytimes.com/2015/06
/13/us/after-freddie-gray-death-west-baltimores-police-presence-drops-and-
murders-soar.html.

Ostroy, Andy. "The Failure of Occupy Wall Street." *Huffington Post,* May 31,
2012. https://www.huffingtonpost.com/andy-ostroy/the-failure-of-occupy-
wal_b_1558787.html.

Peck, Jennifer H. "Minority Perceptions of Police: A State-of-Art-Review." *Policing: An International Journal on Police Strategies and Management* 38, no. 1 (2015): 173–203.

Pierson, Emma, et al. "A Large Scale Analysis of Racial Disparities in Police Stops Across the United States." *Stanford Open Policing Project Working Paper* (2017). https://5harad.com/papers/traffic-stops.pdf.

Rawls, John. *A Theory of Justice, Revised Edition*. Cambridge, MA: Belknap Press, 1999.

Schmidt, Christopher W. *The Sit-Ins: Protest and Legal Change in the Civil Rights Era*. Chicago: University of Chicago Press, 2018.

Sherriff, Lucy. "White Students Form a Human Shield to Protect Black #Fees-MustFall Protesters from South African Police." *HuffPost UK,* Oct 22, 2015. https://www.huffingtonpost.co.za/entry/white-students-form-human-shield -protect-black-protesters-south-african-police_n_8356054.

Simmons, A. John. "Disobedience and its Objects." *Boston University Law Review* 90, no. 4 (2010): 1805–1831.

Stolberg, Sheryl Gay and Stephen Babcock. "Scenes of Chaos in Baltimore as Thousands Protest Freddie Gray's Death." *New York Times,* April 25, 2015. https://www.nytimes.com/2015/04/26/us/baltimore-crowd-swells-in-protest -of-freddie-grays-death.html.

Taube, Aaron. "Maybe Occupy Wall Street Wasn't such a Failure After All." *Business Insider,* September 17, 2013. https://www.businessinsider.com/rec onsidering-the-failure-of-occupy-wall-street-2013-9.

The Negro and the American Promise. Television. Boston, MA: WGBH, 1963.

"The Time has Come," *Eyes on the Prize: America's Civil Rights Movement 1954-1985*. Television. Directed by Hampton, Henry. PBS, 1990.

Thomson, Judith Jarvis. "Self-Defense." *Philosophy & Public Affairs* 20, no. 4 (1991): 283–310.

Umoja, Akinyele. *We Will Shoot Back: Armed Resistance in the Mississippi Freedom Movement*. New York: New York University Press, 2013.

Vasilogambros, Matt. "Did Colin Kaepernick's Protest Fail?" *The Atlantic,* August 30, 2016. https://www.theatlantic.com/news/archive/2016/08/colin-kaepernick-protest-nfl/498065/.

Walzer, Michael. "The Young: A Cup of Coffee and a Seat." *Dissent* 7 (1960).

White, Micah. "Occupy and Black Lives Matter Failed. We can either Win Wars or Win Elections." *The Guardian,* August 28, 2017. https://www.the guardian.com/commentisfree/2017/aug/29/why-are-our-protests-failing-and -how-can-we-achieve-social-change-today.

Chapter 3

(Re)Considering Violence

In the early summer of 2019, UK activists embraced a peculiar new approach to confrontations with far-right politicians—they threw milkshakes at them. It's not exactly clear how the tactic, which came to be known as "milkshaking," caught on. It seems to have started with an attack on Tommy Robinson, a parliamentary hopeful and the founder of the English Defence League, a far-right anti-Muslim organization. Over the course of two days, Robinson was hit by milkshakes at two separate campaign stops. First, in Bury, a milkshake was thrown by an unknown assailant. A day later, at a Warrington protest, twenty-three-year-old Danyaal Mahmud threw his milkshake at Robinson.[1]

According to Mahmud, his choice of projectile on that day was pure coincidence. While on his way to an appointment, he happened upon the protest and decided to join.[2] Mahmud was the sole person of Asian descent in the crowd and claims that Robinson singled him out and began attacking him with racist taunts. Provoked, he threw his milkshake at Robinson.[3] Robinson did not buy Mahmud's claim. In a video released after the incident, Robinson claimed he was politically targeted in an attempt to shut down his campaign. He stated, "I so want to win this. No amount of punches, milkshakes, attacks, or anything is going to stop me."[4]

Whatever his intentions, Mahmud's actions sparked a minor movement. Other far-right activists and political figures soon became milkshaking targets. Carl Benjamin, a YouTuber and UK Independence

Party (UKIP) parliamentary candidate was milkshaked. So was Nigel Farage, the Brexit Party leader known in the United States for his close affiliation with President Donald Trump. In one memorable event, Farage was reportedly trapped on his campaign bus surrounded by demonstrators ready to douse him if he emerged. When Trump visited London in June 2019, protesters clashed with Trump supporters and at least one pro-Trump demonstrator was milkshaked.[5]

Predictably, the viral videos and photos of milkshakings generated online controversy. In addition to the usual debates over its morality and efficacy, the internet argued over how to categorize milkshaking: Is throwing a milkshake at someone an act of violence? The reactions of the targets bolstered the view that it is. In a speech, Benjamin accused his milkshakers of "assault."[6] Farage tweeted that the milkshakers were "radicalized."[7] Robinson responded by throwing several punches at Mahmud.[8] Others threatened a violent response if they were targeted; UKIP candidate Mark Meechen tweeted, "Just to be clear, anyone that comes at me with a milkshake will need the straw to eat their meals for the next few months."[9]

It wasn't just the targets and their supporters who characterized milkshaking as violence. Brendan Cox, widower of British Labor MP Jo Cox,[10] tweeted that he opposes milkshaking because it normalizes violence and intimidation.[11] Commenters on his tweet debated whether the act of milkshaking is itself violent. One commenter asserted that in causing someone to fear or suffer (even slight) bodily harm, milkshaking meets the definition of assault, an inherently violent offense. Another disagreed, arguing that milkshaking, though perhaps ill-advised, is not violent because it doesn't cause physical harm beyond getting the victim wet.[12] Paul Crowther, who milkshaked Farage, argued, "It's a right of protest against people like him. The bile and the racism he spouts out in this country is far more damaging than a bit of milkshake to his front."[13]

The police seemed to agree with the targets over how to characterize the incidents. Crowther and several milkshakers were arrested and charged with common assault; Crowther pleaded guilty. Police also attempted to mitigate further incidents. As the tactic exploded in popularity, police requested that a McDonald's in Edinburgh not sell ice cream or milkshakes near a Farage rally. Burger King was accused on social media of inciting violence when, in response to this news, it tweeted, "Dear people of Scotland. We're selling milkshakes all weekend. Have fun."[14] Meanwhile, some leftist demonstrators sought to distance themselves from the milkshakers because of concerns about the use of violence. At a UKIP counter-protest in Totnes, where Benjamin was milkshaked for the third time, organizers condemned the action as at odds with their peaceful protest.[15]

Academics also disagreed about how to characterize the tactic. In an interview by the New Statesman, Ivan Gololobov, a lecturer at the University of Bath working in punk culture and politics, described milkshaking as a "highly captivating non-violent alternative" to a punch.[16] But Benjamin Franks, a senior lecturer in social and political philosophy at the University of Glasgow, told HuffPostUK that "opponents of this intervention rightly point out that although comical, throwing a milkshake is a form of violence. However, it needs to be borne in mind that it is a very minor form of violence."[17]

So, is milkshaking violent or not? Because violence is often seen as a nonstarter, when people disagree about whether a protest is violent, they are often disagreeing about whether it is justified (or is even an act of protest at all, as opposed to rioting or revolution). In our view, these questions can and should come apart. Whether an act is violent does not determine whether it is justified as protest. Nevertheless, because there is such deep disagreement about what violence is and isn't, we must say something about our understanding of violence. This clarifies what we are defending when we defend the permissibility of violent protest. That said, this chapter does not aim to establish *the* definitive account of violence. That kind of conceptual ground-clearing is beyond our scope. Nor are we attempting to proscribe for activists, who might find a broader conception of violence more amenable to their particular political goals. Instead, we introduce a conception of violence that roughly tracks ordinary usage (with some refinements) and defend it as theoretically and practically useful for our purposes.

AN ORDINARY CONCEPTION OF VIOLENCE

At first glance, violence is any physical attack against a person. However, such an account is clearly inadequate for capturing everything violence is. Surely, at least some attacks against animals and other non-persons are properly characterized as violent. Furthermore, contemporary discussions of protest often include property destruction among descriptions of the violence. Arson, defacing buildings, breaking windows, etc., are all characterized as violent, despite the fact that such actions need not, and often do not, physically harm, hurt, or injure any individuals.

The inclusion of property destruction in the concept of violence is not surprising, given that property is commonly viewed as an extension of the body in traditional liberal theory.John Locke, who first asserts that rights to life, liberty, and property are all of equal importance, argues that a physical attack against a man's property is akin to an attack against his person and should be taken as seriously.[18] Property is often linked to people's livelihoods, and so attacking property is a way of threatening people's lives. Despite critiques of this tight link between bodily integrity and property[19] in both philosophical literature and mainstream social activism, it maintains a firm hold on the popular (and legal) imagination. As U.S. Stand Your Ground-type laws attest, attacks against a person's property are regarded as being close, if not identical, to attacks against their body, and so are taken to legitimate responding accordingly.[20]

It is also unclear that violence must be physical as opposed to psychological or emotional. Following Iris Marion Young, we might posit a spectrum of violence that includes harassment, intimidation, and ridicule. These do not violate an individual's bodily integrity (even broadly construed to include property) and yet seem similar to physical violence.[21] For example, Michelle Carter repeatedly encouraged her supposed friend Conrad Roy to kill himself via phone and text message over a period of weeks. In their final exchange, Carter reportedly told a scared Roy to reenter his carbon-monoxide-filled vehicle after he got out. Roy was later found dead in his truck from the lethal fumes.[22] This is an egregious, but not unique, instance of cyber-bullying, which seems a kind of psychological violence. In addition, intimate partner violence is often marked by manipulation and other forms of cognitive or emotional abuse. It is not obvious that these cases should be considered distinct from physical abuse simply because they are directed at the mental rather than the corporeal.

To bring together these multiple lines of thought, we adopt Robert Audi's three-part definition of violence. According to Audi,

Violence is the physical attack upon, or the vigorous physical abuse of, or the vigorous physical struggle against, a person or animal; or the highly vigorous psychological abuse of, or the sharp, caustic psychological attack upon, a person or animal; or the highly vigorous, or incendiary, or malicious and vigorous, destruction or damaging of property or potential property.[23]

On his view, "violence to animate beings tends to involve or cause their suffering or injury or both."[24] This account helpfully specifies and extends the intuition with which we began. It includes attacks on both persons and property and clarifies that violence doesn't include all of the many ways in which we could seriously harm one another. His account highlights violence as a kind of action—a way in which the abuse is meted out. If it is a particularly vigorous attack, then it deserves to be categorized as violence. By contrast, subtle manipulation over time, like gaslighting or slow poisoning, can be harmful, perhaps even deadly, but not violent (except as a legal description).

That Audi's account characterizes violence as an abuse or an attack is a central feature. Violence is not just any kind of physical or psychological inference, but those that tend toward harm. This distinction, between violence and other forms of interference, is often captured by contrasting violence with a morally neutral concept of force.[25] Whereas force can be applied to one's body (and perhaps even one's mind) without malice, and can even be intended beneficially, violent acts tend toward their object's injury, damage, or harm.[26] This says something central about our conception of violence—that it is normative. To call something violence is to express, perhaps defeasible, moral approbation or concern. Thus, as we noted above, in disputes about violence, interlocutors are frequently actually arguing about whether or not some act was wrong, under the guise of arguing about whether it was violent.

More strongly, some have argued that violence is a term of condemnation. Violence is often a catch-all term for perceived unjust and immoral uses of force. While not denying that "violence" can and often does act as a kind of rhetorical tool, the distinction between violence and force is not whether a particular act is justified or unjustified, but between normative and descriptive understandings. Force is morally neutral whereas violence is at least prima facie wrong. Of course, prima facie wrongness doesn't entail all-things-considered wrongness: we can acknowledge that, as Audi notes, the U.S. nuclear attack on Hiroshima was violent, regardless of whether it was justified.[27]

Subjectivity and Ideology

One major worry for this view is that it builds in a kind of subjectivity to violence, which Audi himself acknowledges. What constitutes vigorous psychological or physical abuse or an attack will in part depend on one's view of what is appropriate, or proper, in a given context, which can vary. Many cases are clear-cut, but some are not. Is deriding an employee with a scathing tone psychological violence? It partially depends on what actions we think are appropriate in a particular workplace.[28] Audi asks whether riding a horse to the point of exhaustion—without whipping or hitting—is violent, and concludes that people will disagree here, depending on their views about the proper treatment of horses.[29] Because our judgments about violence in marginal cases are linked to our judgments about situational appropriateness in those same cases, Audi admits that they will be somewhat subjective. He ameliorates this concern to some extent by pointing out that "the clearer it becomes that what was done qualifies as *vigorous* . . . abuse, the more natural it is to speak of violence."[30] This allows that judgments about violence can and do operate independently of our perception of what is proper in any given situation. But what we perceive as vigorous is also subjective in precisely the same way; Audi concludes that such subjectivity is simply built into our understanding of violence, and so it is impossible to eradicate completely on any ordinary conception.

Unlike Audi, who treats this as a potential problem, we regard it as a feature of the account rather than a bug. Perceptions of violence are often subjective, but not in the sense that they are just up to the individual, or that what violence is simply differs from culture to culture. Rather, they are guided by ideologies like racism and sexism. In recent work, Sally Haslanger argues that ideology consists of more than just a set of shared false beliefs and errors in reasoning. It is best understood as a cultural resource and a source of beliefs that includes, among other things, "a language, a set of concepts, a responsiveness to particular features of things (and not others), [and] a set of social meanings."[31] It "includes psychological mechanisms—cognitive, conative, perceptual, agentic—that sort, shape, and filter what can be the objects of our attitudes."[32] These are, as she puts it, "the very tools that our language and culture provides us in order to think."[33]

Ideology[34] thus influences our perceptions of violence. It causes us to see certain actions as "vigorous" (where vigorous is construed as especially forceful, quick, energetic, or strong—all perceptions that might trigger an immediate response) when they are performed by one social group rather than another. For example, do the actions of a black man and a white man both reaching for their wallets while approaching a police officer mean the same thing in our culture? Plausibly, interpreted through the lens of a shared racist ideology that shapes our perceptions, the answer is "no." One signals a threat, while the other does not. In this way, existent practices that treat black people as violent and threatening give rise to a social context in which such gestures really are threatening.

Recognizing that our subjective perceptions of the tones and valences of actions are infected in this way highlights that our perceptions of what is proper in any given context might be similarly infected by ideologies that, for example, hyper-regulate the actions of black people. This is precisely what we want an account of violence to capture. It alerts us to the fact that the precise nature of violence, if there is one, may be obscured by the dominant ideologies in a culture. So, we should be wary of accounts that attempt to erase this subjectivity. Rather, it is only by emphasizing these perceptual, cultural characteristics of violence that we can craft the tools to resist oppression.

In the case of police brutality, our understanding of violence and attendant concepts like "threatening" and "rioting" may, in some instances, be wrapped up in the very injustice which protesters are attempting to address. Activists point out how the same kinds of behaviors, alternatively undertaken by black protesters and by white sports fans after a team's victory or loss, are policed and portrayed by media outlets in very different ways.[35] In the case of the former, officers dress in military-style garb and the protesters are depicted as "violent" and "criminal." In the latter, police wear normal uniforms and the fans are shown as "revelrous" or "reckless," but not dangerous. One explanation for these disparate responses is that police and media practices are guided by and give rise to a web of meanings within which "black" and "threatening" or "violent" are closely tied together. But those associations can be changed. As Haslanger notes, dominant cultural practices can be disrupted through public challenge and novel experiences.[36] For example, a viral video presenting pictures and videos of black protesters and white sports fans could help us to see both in a new light.[37]

CHALLENGING AN ORDINARY CONCEPTION

So far, we have refined Audi's view to include a discussion of ideology. However, one might think an ordinary language conception is the wrong way to analyze violence, given that people use, understand, and examine violence in so many different ways. Vittorio Bufacchi argues that we are actually operating with (at least) two distinct concepts of violence: Broadly, violence as physical force (introduced above) and violence as violation. The first is a more restrictive view, on which violence is reserved for "physical force deliberately used to cause suffering or injury."[38] The latter is more permissive and admits categories like structural and psychological violence, which violate rights whether or not they are deliberate or physical.

Audi's view is a middle ground between the two concepts because it includes psychological violence. However, it is closer to the force conception in that it locates the essence of violence in vigorous abuse rather than violation (vigorous or not). It is subject to the challenge that it privileges a particular kind of interpersonal phenomenon over much more serious structural and institutional (political) harms. Given that our goal is to arrive at a conception of violence that applies to the political sphere, and that does not unfairly stymie the efforts of the oppressed, such challenges must be taken seriously. In this section, we look at two alternative conceptions of violence—violence as a rights violation and violence as a violation of integrity—that purport to conceptualize violence more structurally. We defend the ordinary language conception over them, while taking on board some important insights about the emancipatory potential of violence.

Violence as a Rights Violation

Viewing an act as violent anytime it violates another's basic rights is appealing, because it allows us to talk in terms of structural violence. It helps to erase moral and conceptual distinctions between the kinds of tools that are usually available to the oppressed—that is, isolated instances of physical resistance, such as throwing bottles and bricks at police, burning draft cards, etc.,—and those available to states and corporations—that is, denial of needed aid, predatory loans, police and military occupations, and strategic silencings. This rights-based conception facilitates talk of covert violence, institutional violence, quiet violence, epistemic violence, and slow violence, none of which need involve any aggressive physical force against persons or properties. In explaining the implications of this conception of violence, Newton Garver argues,

> The fact [is] that there is a black ghetto in most American cities which operates very like any system of slavery. Relatively little violence is needed to keep the institution going and yet the institution entails a real violation of the human beings involved, because they are systematically denied the options which are obviously open to the vast majority of the members of the society in which they live. A systematic denial of options is one way to deprive men of autonomy. If I systematically deprive a person of the options that are normal in our society, then he is no longer in a position to decide for himself what to do. Any institution which systematically robs certain people of rightful options generally available to others does violence to those people.[39]

In his first use of the term "violence" in this passage, Garver is invoking the more ordinary sense of it as a physical attack that tends to cause injury, damage, or harm. But by the end of the passage, he concludes that even without physical attacks, there can be rights violations which are a kind of violence. He continues,

> The institutional form of quiet violence operates when people are deprived of choices in a systematic way by the very manner in which transactions normally take place, without any individual act being violent in itself or any individual decision being responsible for the system.[40]

The worry with thinking about violence purely as a rights violation is that it tends to collapse all unjustified harms into violence. Joseph Betz writes, "If violence is violating a person or a person's rights, then every social wrong is a violent one, every crime against another a violent crime, every sin against one's neighbor an act of violence."[41] If taken purely as a critique of how Garver is broadening our ordinary language conception of violence, this is not particularly compelling, as this is Garver's express aim. Garver contends,

Such a richer perspective is vitally necessary, because we cannot do anything about the violence in our society unless we see it, and most of us do
not see it very well. Conceptions and perceptions are closely dependent
on one another, and perhaps having a better idea of what violence is will
enable us to recognize more readily the many sorts of violence that sur-
round our lives.[42]

Garver is expressly attempting a counter-ideological move: he is centering structures rather than individual actors. He aims to bring about
a perceptual change by arguing for a conceptual change. And such
perceptual changes *are* vitally necessary—they are one of the crucial
activities of protest. Imagine a world in which we were inclined to see
violence first in the institutional structures that produce conditions of
scarcity for some, causing physical harm through starvation and disease, and only derivatively in the forceful, physical attacks committed
by individuals. Such a powerful conceptual shift could lead to profound
social change and is thus an obvious candidate for an emancipatory
conception of violence.

Nevertheless, we resist taking up this view for two reasons, one
theoretical and one practical. Theoretically, this move simply goes
too far. It renders incoherent calls for violent revolution or violent
defense in the face of injustice, because no one's rights are violated
when the revolution or defense is justified. Therefore, according to
this view, all well-targeted responses to injustice are necessarily
nonviolent. But this seems weird: surely it is important to maintain
the distinction between nonviolent and violent responses to oppression. This allows us to draw out one central function of violence,
namely, that it can upset ideologies in ways that are justified and
necessary.

Practically, we need an account that will allow us to talk meaning-
fully about a particular phenomenon that is a source of controversy in
protests. When people worry about violence in protest, they are almost
always talking about the use of excessive force that causes injury, damage, and harm, whether or not they believe that rights were violated. In
this sense, our analysis of violence is conservative. We err on the side of
how "violence" is used in ordinary language, rather than redefining it.
This is because our goal is to encourage people to step back from their
initial reactions to nonlethal violent protest. We don't wish to define
away their worries, but rather persuade them to see it in a new light.

In thinking about how to adjudicate between different conceptions, we take seriously the view that concepts are tools that allow us to navigate our world and coordinate our activities. This can move us to revise our concepts when we find them to be ill-suited to goals of justice, but it can also alert us to times when maintaining a particular usage, though imprecise, will allow us to communicate with an audience and potentially convince them to support those just ends.

Structural Violence

Still, it is essential to capture the insight that violence is a structural, as well as an interpersonal, phenomenon. On the one hand, Audi's focus on violence as it is committed by individuals is helpful since it centers precisely the kind of violence that is often undertaken by protesters who lack the power to enact violence at a structural level. It focuses our attention on the relevant phenomena we wish to defend. On the other hand, if that focus on interpersonal violence obscures other sources of violence—particularly violence as it is enacted at a structural level— then the definition does a great disservice, since activists are often attempting to draw our attention to structural oppression, and defending their uses of interpersonal violence by reference to that structural violence.

Structural violence, as Garver characterizes it, is the unequal life chances, or restrictions to autonomy, that arise from the normal functioning of institutions and for which no individual is responsible. While an ordinary language conception like ours is not able to capture this as violence, it doesn't need to. We have a perfectly serviceable concept—oppression—which does. As Iris Marion Young writes, "In the most general sense, all oppressed people suffer some inhibition of their ability to develop and exercise their capacities and express their needs, thoughts and feelings."[43] Oppression is structural rather than individual because it results not from the intentions of any individual tyrant but from the everyday habits and norms of well-intentioned people. As she writes, oppression is the result of "the normal processes of everyday life."[44] This seems to capture precisely what Garver has in mind and so it is unclear why we ought to substitute "violence" for "oppression." Furthermore, violence plays a central role in Young's theory, as one of her "five faces" of oppression, which suggests that this substitution would be a kind of category mistake.[45]

Violence is not oppression but it is related to oppression. While acts of violence themselves are committed by individuals, Young's insight is that some acts of violence are social practices—they exist in a social context which "makes them possible and even acceptable."[46] This does not mean that violence is structural in the absurd sense that a structure somehow lashes out at a person. Rather, violence is structural in that it is directed at members of social groups because they are members of those groups. Their position in the social structure makes them vulnerable to violence: they are schematized as threats, or as apt for certain kinds of treatment. In this way, "wife-beating" is not a random occurrence. It is a social practice. In a patriarchal society, women qua women can threaten a man's position in the social hierarchy—his masculine identity—and that position can be reaffirmed through hurting women. Transwomen, in particular, are victims of this social practice. Even if we condemn it in individual cases, we also participate in maintaining the social context which makes it intelligible as a viable means for men to assert their social position. The violence is structural because it is rendered meaningful as an action by its embeddedness in a social context.

The full meaning of violence can only be understood, then, if we recognize that violence is always situated within a social context. Without such an appreciation, we lose the full valence of the action. The subjective features of Audi's account can accommodate this structural insight by centering the notion that violence is best understood as embedded within social structures that render certain actions meaningful. The subjectivity of violence is not random, but ideological; it tracks the oppressive social practices of a given culture. This has an important upshot for the normativity of violence. We have to pay attention to who typically gets demonized (black civilians) and who typically gets lauded (police officers) in any violent scenario.

Of course, even this refined ordinary language conception of violence will not capture all violations, or deliberate attempts to cause injury, damage, or harm. Many cases of sexual and psychological abuse are not violent on this account, even as they are horrific, injurious attacks on victims. Young explicitly warns against attempts to reduce all oppression to some common descriptor and it is unclear why we should disregard that warning, at least at the level of theory. At the level of practice though, there may well be compelling reasons to do so. (The phrase "Silence is Violence" might be reductionist but has great rhetorical power.) However, focusing on this usage for the purposes of talking to a particular audience reveals something significant about the interplay between violence and power that might be obscured if we were to switch wholly to the broader "violence as a rights violation" conception.

Violence as a Violation of Integrity

The final challenge that we consider to this refined ordinary language conception of violence comes from Bufacchi. He argues that vigorous abuse is merely a symptom, rather than the essence, of violence.[47] Like us, he rejects the view that violence is necessarily a term of condemnation, as in the "violence as a rights violation" view that we discussed above. Rather than capturing all and only instances of rights violations or unjust harms, Bufacchi argues that violence is a violation of integrity. He understands integrity as a non-normative concept of wholeness or intactness. As he says, "The term 'integrity' here simply refers to something that has not been broken, or that has not lost its original form."[48] Per his analysis,

> an act of violence is fundamentally a violation of integrity, to the extent that it damages or destroys a pre-existing unity. It may be easier to see this violation of unity in terms of violence against an inanimate object, although the same violation also applies to people and other animals. When a bomb falls on a house reducing it to a heap of rubble, a process of transformation as degradation takes place which alters the pre-existing entity of the structure as a house. Similarly, when a person becomes the victim of an act of violence, it is one's integrity as a person that is being infringed, since in the process of being violated one is reduced to a lesser being, in physical and/or psychological terms.[49]

Like other theories of violence as a violation, this expands the scope of violence. But it does so without committing to the claim that rights are at the heart of violence. Violation of rights can occur without a violation of integrity (and violations of integrity can occur without a violation of rights, as in self-defense). And helpfully, unlike violations of rights, the violation of integrity is not wrong by definition. Yet, it still centers the experience of the victim in the account, describing violence in terms of its impact, rather than in terms of the actions of the perpetrator.

To demonstrate the advantages of this view over one in which violence is a kind of force, Bufacchi gives the example of sexual violence, a term which (according to the CDC[50]) describes all non-consensual or coercive sexual activity. Bufacchi sees great utility in the fact that his theory can accommodate all such cases as violent. Drawing on Susan Brison's work on the effects of sexual (and other) trauma on personal identity, Bufacchi argues that his account makes sense of victims' descriptions of the effects of sexual abuse as the destruction of an intact self. On his interpretation, the self is a preexisting unity that can be destroyed by sexual violence, whether such abuse is "vigorous" or "sharp" or "caustic" or not, by undermining the victim's capacity for agency, and estranging them from—or trapping them in—their body.

This view is appealing in part because it can capture such ostensibly diverse experiences as being of a kind.[51] However, taking up this position means that Bufacchi has to explain why violence is wrong when it is wrong, and this explanation must be linked to his understanding of integrity. To do so, Bufacchi argues that some violations of integrity are humiliating, and when they are humiliating, they are distinctively, intrinsically bad and prima facie wrong.[52] Humiliation, in his sense, is a normative and social notion, as opposed to psychological. That a person *feels* humiliated is insufficient; what matters is whether they are the victims of "maltreatment based on unequal power relations consisting in domination."[53] Wrongful acts of violence, then, are ones in which the perpetrator asserts power over the victim: they mistreat the victim by rendering the victim vulnerable to them.[54] A person is humiliated when they are either brought lower than they were before the violence—lower in relation to their previous status—or brought below the level of the perpetrator. It is not merely the state of being powerless or vulnerable, which may accompany death or other natural harms, that is most troubling about violence. Humiliation is a distinctly social harm, unique to violence, and the core of Bufacchi's account of the wrongness of violence.

There is thus a relationship between violence and injustice. Not all injustice is violence, according to Bufacchi, but his theory of violence, and why it is bad and wrong (when it is), points to what is bad and wrong about injustice.[55] The power relations of domination and subordination are humiliating, because they make some people vulnerable and powerless in relation to others. This insight that injustice cannot be fully captured in terms of some unfair distribution of material resources or violation of rights is not new; Bufacchi's central point is his analysis of oppressive social relations as humiliating, via his account of violence. As he writes, "The act of violence is an act of . . . humiliation, and [so] to be humiliated becomes an issue of injustice."[56]

Notice that on Bufacchi's view, humiliation is an objective state rather than a felt experience. However, in attempting to explain the wrongness of injustice in terms of such "objective" humiliation, Bufacchi both misses and occludes what is most distinctive about structural injustice—the ways in which injustice shapes individual agency, creating and molding preferences and obstacles such that our powerlessness and vulnerability often feel natural or accidental rather than human-made. This identity formation is not merely the result of repressive institutions or other agents, but also arises from the subtler forces of culture. Focusing on the experiences of its victims, Haslanger distinguishes between these two oppressive forces. In the former, the subordinated "participate unwillingly and experience [their oppression] as repressive."[57] In the latter, oppression is "enacted unthinkingly or even willingly by the subordinated or privileged."[58] It is oppression by ideology.

Ideology obscures the experiences of oppressed groups, at times even from the groups themselves. For example, without alternative notions of what women can do, a patriarchal ideology limits women to the roles of housewife and mother, and women who are subject to that ideology will perceive such roles as natural and appropriate, rather than oppressive. Even in cases where the oppressed group comes to understand their situation as oppressive, ideology can suppress uptake of that understanding by others. When certain social hierarchies are regarded as natural, the oppressed will have a more difficult time explaining why the policies that perpetuate them ought to change. Meanwhile, stereotypes of oppressed groups as irrational (or stupid, or naive) make it difficult for them to advocate publicly on their own behalf.[59] By determining the tools of thought that are easily available, ideology sustains the hierarchical social order.

In doing so, ideology also sets, to some degree, what is rational for people to do in relation to others. As Haslanger says, when thinking about agency under conditions of oppression, "The starting point of inquiry is not an abstract agent, but individuals with minds and bodies that have been shaped by interactions with others and whose actions are meaningful primarily within social practices."[60] To go back to patriarchal ideology, what it is to be a wife is to keep a clean house-hold, prepare food, and emotionally support your spouse. This cultur-ally specific social meaning "constrain[s] what's considered possible or intelligible," and influences people's perceptions.[61] We use these cultural-conceptual tools to shape our practices.[62] That a person is a wife gives them a reason to care about the mess in the living room or what time supper is on the table apart from any external influences like their level of hunger. Why do they plan the meals, or make the grocery list, or direct their husband in the kitchen? Partly, it is because they have time, or know what is needed, or are the more skilled cook. But it is also because they are a wife and that is what wives do. So, this social meaning is part of the basis of their agency, where agency is acting for reasons. Practices are the well-worn paths through which agency flows.[63] Ideology explains how we can willingly come to enact oppressive structures and why we have reason to do so. As Haslanger concludes, "Ideology . . . is a kind of barrier to social justice, one that ultimately affects our agency 'from within.'"[64]

In oppressive circumstances of this sort, it is not rational, in many cases, to feel humiliated. Operating within the social practices that are available to us, we experience ourselves as making choices and exercis-ing our agency, even when those same practices oppress us. Part of the insidiousness of oppression is its ability to create powerlessness and vulnerability that feels natural, rather than humiliating or degrading. Bufacchi attempts to elide this worry by appealing to an ideal "Specta-tor" to make sense of the claim that oppressed people can be the victims of violence, and so, humiliated, regardless of how they feel.[65] However, by doing so, he fails to explain injustice in terms of the actual integrity-violating impact on its victims.

Recall that for Bufacchi, integrity is descriptive. It posits the self as a preexisting unity (like a building that could be destroyed), but precisely what Haslanger points out is that the self is at least partially socially constituted. So, if Bufacchi wants to maintain a descriptive understand-ing of integrity in explaining the badness and wrongness of both vio-lence and injustice, he must regard people's integrity as constituted (at least partially) by their actual practices and relations, not as it might be regarded by an ideal spectator. What is humiliating, then, depends on how you reason from within the practices that make you who you are (not on how you might reason from nowhere). If, by contrast, he moves to this more normative understanding of integrity, he loses the ability to make sense of, for example, Brison's account of the impact of sexual violence as a violation of integrity, because for Brison too, the self is partially socially constituted. Her description of the impact of sexual violence depends on an understanding of the self as relational. Either Bufacchi must accept that some structural injustice is not humiliating (because it does not offend against people's actual agential practices), or he must give up his purely descriptive notion of integrity. Regardless, his account ends up occluding the badness and wrongness of oppression. It leads us to miss violence and injustice when they are present and to see violence as wrong even when it may not be.

In fact, it is because our agency is a social agency that not all violence is humiliating, even when it is wrong, because not all wrongful violence is a threat to our existing social relations and status. Some instances of violence perform precisely the opposite function, alerting society that those involved are worthy of respect and reinforcing their status. Consider duels, where agreeing to fight is a way of confirming the status of one's opponent as a person deserving of the opportunity to defend their honor. Irrespective of the outcome, humiliation is avoided, and social respect is restored, by engaging in the contest.[66] Or, think of soldiers and freedom fighters who might experience a sense of fortitude, rather than humiliation, when wounded. Depending on the nature of the conflict and their commitment to it, such a reaction isn't obviously irrational, though the violation of their integrity is evident, as is the accompanying physical and psychological damage and, again, depending on the circumstances, the wrongness of the violence.

The same problem also appears with less serious violations of integrity. Is being punched hard in the arm by one's younger sibling for hogging their videogame humiliating? Probably not, though it may leave one with a bad bruise and a sense of irritation. In linking humiliation to the wrongness of violence, Bufacchi discounts the fact that whether or not such feelings occur—and are rational—in the face of violence is determined by whether and how we (and importantly, others) contextualize the event within our preexisting social hierarchy. While emphasizing humiliation as the distinctly social harm of violence, Bufacchi ignores how the social may intervene to mitigate or even erase that harm. Consequently, when violence is expected, constrained to a particular context, nonlethal, and/or causes little or no lasting physical or psychological harm, then the feelings of powerless and vulnerability to others may not arise or, if they do, they may not be rational. This can occur even when the violence is wrongful.

Similarly, not all humiliating violence is obviously wrong. In oppressive societies, some humiliation might be justified, when it is used to right or combat an oppressive social relation. Having one's status lowered is not always wrong, although it is humiliating. Bufacchi seems to take for granted that there is a rough parity of status between the victim and the perpetrator, such that a reduction of the victim's status will always place them in a lower, unjustified position. But in situations of oppression, there isn't status parity, and that is precisely the problem. If violence is capable of lowering the status of certain individuals, it could actually create parity by puncturing their invulnerability and reducing their outsized power in relation to others.[67] So, violence is a potentially formidable tool for social justice, and one which we should not dismiss out of hand.

RETURN TO MILKSHAKING

Bufacchi does give us an important insight here; just not the one he thought he was giving us. That violence can be humiliating without being wrong informs our refined ordinary language conception of violence. By including an account of the importance of ideology, we see that vigorous attacks and/or abuse always depend on our subjective understandings of what is occurring. Our ideologically infected social practices lead us to see the world in certain ways, and so we must be cautious when identifying and judging violence. By including an account of social relations and social agency under conditions of oppression, we see that the injury, damage, and harm that violence causes can be socially situated. This leads us to conclude that violence, when it is humiliating, has emancipatory potential.

To see when and how this might work in practice, we return to the case of milkshaking. Milkshaking, depending on how it is carried out, could be violent. Whether tossed from close range or lobbed from a distance, throwing a milkshake is a vigorous physical action. It is also intentional and so properly understood as an attack. More controversial is whether milkshaking is an act that tends to cause injury, damage, or harm to its target. To our knowledge, none of those who were hit by milkshakes were actually physically harmed. However, following Audi, an act of violence does not require that someone is harmed (nor is the fact that someone is harmed sufficient), only that the action is of a sort that tends to cause injury, damage, or harm.[68] The use of semi-frozen projectiles could cross that threshold.

Here, some people will disagree. As we mentioned earlier, at least one online commenter argued that milkshaking cannot be violence because it causes no physical harm to its target other than getting them wet. Part of this disagreement could rest on how the milkshaking is performed. Demonstrators used various techniques, some throwing the entire cup while others emptied its contents onto their targets. We contend that the former crosses into violence, while the latter is a far more ambiguous case.

Milkshakes and the cups they are served in can be quite solid and the force with which they are thrown quite hard. Think of throwing snowballs, which usually do not cause injury when thrown by children at other children who are wearing thick winter clothing. But, thrown by adults dressed in casual wear, snowballs could easily and expectedly cause small welts or bruises. The potential for snowballs to cause injury is captured in our common reaction to them, which is to duck and cover unprotected parts, like our heads. In doing so, we acknowledge the potential for injury and seek to avoid it. So, in general, throwing a milkshake while it is encased in a cup is an act of violence, albeit a minor one.

Emptying a milkshake onto a target is less clearly violent. A relevant comparison might be to glitter bombing, a protest tactic used primarily by LGBTQ+ activists, in which a target has handfuls of glitter thrown on them. In contrast to being threatened with snowballs, the most evasive action one is likely to take when being glitter-bombed is closing one's eyes and mouth. While injury is certainly possible (one could get glitter in their eye, for example) it is neither expected nor is it the point. At most, one is likely to suffer the annoyance of finding glitter in unexpected places for weeks to come.

One could argue that any type of milkshaking tends to cause psychological harm and so, counts as violence. Milkshaking was a relatively short-lived and isolated phenomenon (lasting about four months in total and occurring perhaps a dozen times) and it is impossible to know for sure the mental effects on the targets, as they were motivated to either overstate the effects to gain sympathy or understate them to preserve their images as tough guys. We do know however, that milkshaking, like all violence, occurs in a social context, not in a blank void. So, we can consider its likely psychological harms, given the relevant social meanings, practices, and hierarchies. In particular, milkshaking has the potential to be humiliating.

Recall that Nigel Farage was the target of milkshaking on several occasions. His first milkshaking occurred in Newcastle at the hands of Paul Crowther. Pictures of the event showed Farage in a dark suit splattered in white milkshake. Crowther was tackled by Farage's security team and subsequently arrested. As they ushered him away, Farage purportedly berated his bodyguards for failing to anticipate and protect him from the milkshake attack. Later that week, he reportedly refused to leave his bus at a campaign stop when protesters were spotted nearby, dressed in black, wearing balaclavas, and holding milkshakes.[69] He left the bus briefly to meet supporters, but stayed close to it.[70] Farage's anger at his bodyguards and hesitation to exit the bus suggest that Farage may have found the experience of being milkshaked humiliating.

While milkshaking had already been established as a symbol of condemnation of right-wing political candidates accused of bigotry, the attack on Farage was the first time the tactic was used against a prominent politician. As a career politician, leader (and former leader) of two prominent third parties, and Brexit figurehead, Farage represents for progressives a mainstreaming of nationalist, anti-immigrant, and anti-Islam policies. While arguments for Brexit were often made on the grounds of economic advantage or political sovereignty, they also appealed to cultural preservation and scarcity of resources in ways that, when not straightforwardly racist or anti-Islam, were tinged with racial undertones. Farage, in particular, walked this line. He argued that Great Britain should accept refugees from Syria's Christian minority rather than its majority Muslim population. During the Brexit campaign, he unveiled a billboard depicting a long line of brown-skinned migrants with the words, "We must break free of the EU and take back control."

However, he also condemned those further to the right, like his fellow milkshaking victim, Tommy Robinson. He claimed Robinson was too extreme in his anti-Islam views, and left the UKIP party (of which he was the founder and former leader) when Robinson was appointed as an advisor in it. And, unlike Robinson and Carl Benjamin, who responded to being milkshaked or to the threat of milkshaking with violence or threats of violence, Farage simply walked away while his bodyguards tackled the milkshaker. He later tweeted, "Sadly some remainers have become radicalised, to the extent that normal campaigning is becoming impossible. For a civilised democracy to work you need the losers' consent, politicians not accepting the referendum result have led us to this."[71] Farage's tweet appeals to the values of a democratic society to condemn the milkshakers, placing them outside of it.

The danger that Farage represents is the normalization and promotion of xenophobia in mainstream political discourse. In the wake of an interview in which Farage implied that Brexit was necessary because an influx of migrants would leave British women vulnerable to sexual assault,[72] three women from across the political spectrum drafted an open letter condemning his remarks and calling on him to apologize.[73] They accused Farage of violating liberal rules of discourse, arguing, "Veiled threats of sexual assault by a new immigrant community stray too close for comfort to the race hate laws, and certainly cross the line of civilised discourse and rational debate."[74] The archbishop of Canterbury, Justin Welby, agreed, saying,

> I think that [Farage's comment] is an inexcusable pandering to people's worries and prejudices. That is giving legitimisation to racism which I've seen in parishes in which I've served, and has led to attacks on people in those parishes. We cannot legitimise that.[75]

The success of right-wing politicians in Great Britain, who have followed in Farage's wake, suggest that illiberal ideologies of xenophobia and cultural superiority are becoming acceptable in mainstream political discourse. It is in this context that milkshaking emerged as a tactic for painting politicians, like Farage, as fools.

Milkshaking is appropriate in this context precisely because of its humiliating potential. It has the effect of making those on the far right, whose policies represent a dangerous, terrifying, oppressive future, look silly. It's also juvenile. Such an immature response invites one to see both victims and perpetrators in a less serious light. This effect is far more devastating for the politicians, who are attempting to appear serious, than for the protesters, who make no such claims.[76] "Milkshake on a figure who pretends to be serious and well-established has become an incredibly powerful image destroying the platform of seriousness," says Gololobov. He continues, "Milkshake on a fancy suit of an upper middle-class bigot symbolises how fake their bravado is and how irrational their arguments are—not far from school bullying. And what is the best way to stop the bully? It is to show them their place.''[77] Whether or not it succeeded, milkshaking has the potential, via its humiliating function, to expose someone like Farage as a laughable figure rather than a serious politician. It takes him down a peg, deservedly so.[78]

Of course, not all humiliations produce social parity. Andy Ngo's attack at a Proud Boys rally shows the potential of milkshaking to go wrong. The Proud Boys are a self-described "Western Chauvinist" organization.[79] When they marched in Portland in June 2019, they were met by counter-demonstrators, including some who attacked Ngo. Ngo was punched in the face by one demonstrator, approached aggressively by several others, and perhaps kicked by another. Milkshake was tossed onto Ngo several times, and thrown at him in cups, even as he retreated. Protesters sprayed him with silly string, aiming for his head and face.[80] As he fled, protesters followed him, throwing milkshakes and laughing. One yelled, "Fucking owned, bitch."

Ngo sustained injuries including a torn earlobe and bruises and cuts on his face. The actual physical injuries appear to have resulted from the punch, which is obviously violent, and not the milkshake. However, throwing the milkshake in Ngo's face obscured his vision, making him less able to defend himself from subsequent physical attacks. So, throwing a milkshake in this context could tend to cause injury. Moreover, Ngo is a gay, Asian man. Setting aside the physical violence he suffered, Ngo was surrounded by a crowd of white people screaming at him. Even if they take themselves to be defending progressive, antiracist values, this could be more intimidating for Ngo than it would be for a white person. And the use of "bitch" to refer to a gay man could further increase his humiliation and the intimating nature of the attack. Even if the perpetrator knew nothing of Ngo's sexuality, the social meaning of that particular insult, when applied to a gay man, could lead to an added level of fear and insult.

The point is, since the humiliating nature of the violence is dependent on the context in which it occurs, context matters for determining what an attack does to the relevant social relations. We must consider not only the identity and position of the target(s) and the perpetrator(s), but also the ideological milieu in which the violence is deployed. This can prompt us to reflect on when humiliating violence is wrong, and when it might be justified in the fight against oppression in liberal societies.

NOTES

1. Nosheen Iqbal, "'I'm Getting Death Threats,' Says Man Who Threw Milkshake on Tommy Robinson," *The Guardian*, May 5, 2019.

2. Iqbal, "'I'm Getting Death Threats,' Says Man Who Threw Milkshake on Tommy Robinson."

3. Iliana Magra, "Why are Milkshakes being Thrown at Right-Wing Politicians Like Nigel Farage?" *New York Times*, May 21, 2019.

4. Lizzie Dearden, "Tommy Robinson has Milkshake Thrown Over Him for Second Time in Two Days," *Independent UK*, May 2, 2019.

5. Chiara Giordano, "Trump Supporter 'Milkshaked' by Protesters as Tempers Flare Outside Parliament," *Independent UK*, June 4, 2019.

6. Johnny O'Shea, "UKIP Candidate Carl Benjamin in Truro Milkshake Melee," *BBC News*, May 10, 2019.

7. Magra, "Why are Milkshakes being Thrown at Right-Wing Politicians Like Nigel Farage?"

8. Iqbal, "'I'm Getting Death Threats,' Says Man Who Threw Milkshake on Tommy Robinson."

9. Magra, "Why are Milkshakes being Thrown at Right-Wing Politicians Like Nigel Farage?"

10. Jo Cox was shot and killed by a neo-Nazi in a politically motivated attack. Kester Aspden, "The Making of a Bedsit Nazi: Who was the Man Who Killed Jo Cox?" *The Guardian*, Dec 6, 2019.

11. Brendan Cox, *Tweet*, 2019.

12. Cox, *Tweet*.

13. Jennifer Hassan, "Milkshake-Wielding Protesters Trap Nigel Farage on His Brexit Bus," *Washington Post*, May 22, 2019.

14. Hassan, "Milkshake-Wielding Protesters Trap Nigel Farage on His Brexit Bus."

15. Anoosh Chakelian, "'Lactose Against Intolerance!' how Milkshake Became a Tool of Protest," *New Statesman*, May 16, 2019.

16. Chakelian, "'Lactose Against Intolerance!' how Milkshake Became a Tool of Protest."

17. George Bowden, "'Milkshaking': How the Divisive Protest Against Politicians Escalated very Quickly," *HuffPost UK*, May 20, 2019.

18. John Locke, *Two Treatises of Government, and; A Letter Concerning Toleration* (New Haven: Yale University Press, 2004), III.18.

19. David Rodin argues that attacks against a person are intrinsically different from attacks against a person's property. David Rodin, *War and Self-Defense* (Oxford: Oxford University Press, 2002).

20. Tamara Rice Lave, "Shoot to Kill: A Critical Look at Stand Your Ground Laws," *University of Miami Law Review* 67 (2013), 827–57. We aren't

supporting Stand Your Ground laws; we are merely pointing out that their widespread implementation in the United States suggests that the popular view is that physical attacks against property are similar, if not identical, to physical attacks against a person.

21. Iris Marion Young, "Five Faces of Oppression," in *Justice and the Politics of Difference* (New Jersey: Princeton University Press, 1990), 61–3.

22. Alanna Durkin Richer, "Conviction Upheld for Woman Who Urged Boyfriend's Suicide," *AP News*, February 6, 2019.

23. Robert Audi, "On the Meaning and Justification of Violence," in *Violence: Award Winning Essays in the Council for Philosophical Studies Competition*, ed. Jerome A. Shaffer (New York: David McKay, 1971), 59–60.

24. Audi, "On the Meaning and Justification of Violence," 60.

25. See, for example, Ronald B. Miller, "Violence, Force and Coercion," in *Violence; Award Winning Essays in the Council for Philosophical Studies Competition*, ed. Jerome A. Shaffer (New York: David McKay, 1971), 9–44.

26. Miller, "Violence, Force and Coercion," 25.

27. Audi, "On the Meaning and Justification of Violence," 59.

28. Audi, "On the Meaning and Justification of Violence," 67. In addition, such judgments of appropriateness will partially depend on the social positions of the relevant actors.

29. Audi, "On the Meaning and Justification of Violence," 65.

30. Audi, "On the Meaning and Justification of Violence," 66.

31. Sally Haslanger, "Racism, Ideology and Social Movements," *Res Philosophica* 94, no. 1 (2017b), 7.

32. Haslanger, "Racism, Ideology and Social Movements," 16.

33. Haslanger, "Racism, Ideology and Social Movements," 9.

34. We discuss ideology in more detail in chapter 4.

35. See, for example, Derrick Clifton, "11 Stunning Images Highlight the Double Standard of Reactions to Riots Like Baltimore," *The Movement*, April 27, 2015.

36. Haslanger, "Racism, Ideology and Social Movements," 15.

37. *Black Protests Vs. White Riots,* YouTube video, 2:54. Brave New Films, 2015.

38. Vittorio Bufacchi, "Two Concepts of Violence," *Political Studies Review* 3, no. 2 (2005), 197.

39. Newton Garver, "What Violence Is," in *Philosophy for a New Generation, Second Edition*, eds. A. K. Bierman and James A. Gould, 1973), 264.

40. Garver, "What Violence Is," 265.

41. Joseph Betz, "Violence: Garver's Definition and a Deweyan Correction," *Ethics* 87, no. 4 (1977), 341.

42. Garver, "What Violence Is," 265.

43. Young, "Five Faces of Oppression," 41.

44. Young, "Five Faces of Oppression," 41.

45. Young, "Five Faces of Oppression," 39–65.

46. Young, "Five Faces of Oppression," 61.

47. Vittorio Bufacchi, *Violence and Social Justice* (London: Palgrave Macmillan, 2007), 40.

48. Bufacchi, *Violence and Social Justice*, 40.

49. Bufacchi, *Violence and Social Justice*, 41.

50. "Sexual Violence," https://www.cdc.gov/violenceprevention/sexual violence/index.html.

51. This view doesn't distinguish between "violent" rape and rape by virtue of some level of vigor; all rape is violent.

52. Though he does not say this and, indeed, seems to claim the opposite, his view would also appear to entail that not all acts of violence are bad. For example, the demolition of a building is a clear violation of integrity, destroying a preexisting unity and reducing the object to "a lesser being, in physical . . . terms." Bufacchi, *Violence and Social Justice*, 41. But it is not always bad to destroy a building.

53. Bufacchi, *Violence and Social Justice*, 132. Bufacchi borrows this notion of "ascriptive humiliation" from Lukes. Steven Lukes, "Humiliation and the Politics of Identity," *Social Research* 64, no. 1 (Apr 1, 1997), 36–51.

54. As Bufacchi claims, "It is being vulnerable *to* someone, or having our mortality being determined by another person, another mortal, that is the issue. Another way of stating this point is by saying that what is most troubling is not being powerless per se, but being powerless in relation to someone else who has power over us." Bufacchi, *Violence and Social Justice*, 118.

55. Bufacchi, *Violence and Social Justice*, 139.

56. Bufacchi, *Violence and Social Justice*, 132.

57. Sally Haslanger, "I—Culture and Critique," *Aristotelian Society Supplementary Volume* 91, no. 1 (2017a), 150.

58. Haslanger, "I—Culture and Critique," 149.

59. For more on the silencing of oppressed groups, see chapter 1.

60. Sally Haslanger, "Practical Reason and Social Practices," in *The Routledge Handbook of Practical Reason*, eds. Ruth Chang and Kurt Sylvan (New York: Routledge, 2021), section 2.

61. Haslanger, "I—Culture and Critique," 155.

62. Haslanger, "I—Culture and Critique," 155. Thus, the unequal division of household labor persists even as women participate to an equal or greater degree in the labor market. Any number of conscious or unconscious biases may be maintaining this divide, but part of the explanation is cultural.

63. In other words, as Haslanger puts it, "Cultural scripts and narratives create valleys along which agency easily flows." She goes on to point out that "Although it may be easier to flow in the valley, we have choices between valleys, or to climb the peaks instead." Sally Haslanger, "What is a Social Practice?" *Royal Institute of Philosophy Supplement* 82 (2018), 242.

64. Haslanger, "Practical Reason and Social Practices," in section 2.

65. The Spectator's view is the "view-from-nowhere." Bufacchi, *Violence and Social Justice*, 37. This concept was popularized by Thomas Nagel, *The View from Nowhere* (Oxford: Oxford University Press, 1989).

66. Bufacchi might respond that duels are cases of "consensual violence" and so, not captured by his theory, but that seems a stretch. The other examples he provides of consensual violence are sadomasochism and assisted suicide, which are intended to produce pleasure or avoid pain and so, not apt for analysis on a paradigm of humiliation. By contrast, the purpose of duels is to alleviate humiliation by restoring/protecting social status.

67. Bufacchi mentions the possibility of using violence to rectify unequal social relations in situations of oppression, but reduces it to a point about the reclamation of status and identity by the oppressed. Here, he follows Frantz Fanon, whose view we consider in chapter 6. He does not seem to recognize violence's potential to reduce the status of the oppressors.

68. Audi, "On the Meaning and Justification of Violence," 60.

69. Vicky Castle and Will Rider, "Nigel Farage Stuck on His Brexit Bus because People Turned Up with Milkshake," *Kent Live*, May 22, 2019.

70. John Bowden, "Nigel Farage Briefly Stuck on Brexit Bus Surrounded by Protesters with Milkshakes," *The Hill*, May 22, 2019.

71. "Nigel Farage Hit by Milkshake during Newcastle Walkabout." *BBC News,* May 20, 2019b.

72. Jessica Elgot and Rowena Mason, "Nigel Farage: Migrant Sex Attacks to be 'nuclear Bomb' of EU Referendum," *The Guardian*, June 5, 2016.

73. Doreen Lawrence, Sayeda Warsi, and Shami Chakrabarti, "Nigel Farage must Apologise for Sex Attack Warning," *The Guardian*, June 6, 2016.

74. Lawrence, Warsi, and Chakrabarti, "Nigel Farage must Apologise for Sex Attack Warning."

75. Elgot and Mason, "Nigel Farage: Migrant Sex Attacks to be 'nuclear Bomb' of EU Referendum."

76. And in fact, some protesters might want to be seen as having fun and joking around. Laughtivists do this explicitly. Srdja Popovic and Sophia A. McClennen, *Pranksters Vs. Autocrats: Why Dilemma Actions Advance Nonviolent Activism* (Ithaca: Cornell University Press, 2020).

77. Chakelian, "'Lactose Against Intolerance!' how Milkshake Became a Tool of Protest."

78. This is similar to Myisha Cherry's point that anger in response to a wrongdoing can function as an equalizer. She writes, "Perhaps through anger, the angry agent brings the wrongdoer from a position of superiority—from which the wrongdoing occurs—to a position of equality. This equality is not one of pain, but one of status." Myisha Cherry, "Love, Anger, and Racial Injustice," in *The Routledge Handbook on Love in Philosophy*, ed. Adrienne Martin (New York: Routledge, 2019), 160.

79. Zack Beauchamp, "The Assault on Conservative Journalist Andy Ngo, Explained," *Vox*, July 3, 2019.

80. This is pulled from live video footage. *Conservative Writer Andy Ngo Roughed Up at Portland Antifa/Right Wing Protests*, YouTube. The Oregonian, 2019a: https://www.youtube.com/watch?v=8WzMZxT-41k.

BIBLIOGRAPHY

Aspden, Kester. "The Making of a Bedsit Nazi: Who was the Man Who Killed Jo Cox?" *The Guardian,* Dec 6, 2019. http://www.theguardian.com/news/2019/dec/06/bedsit-nazi-man-killed-jo-cox-thomas-mair.

Audi, Robert. "On the Meaning and Justification of Violence." In *Violence: Award Winning Essays in the Council for Philosophical Studies Competition*, edited by Jerome A. Shaffer, 45–99. New York: David McKay, 1971.

Beauchamp, Zack. "The Assault on Conservative Journalist Andy Ngo, Explained." *Vox,* July 3, 2019. https://www.vox.com/policy-and-politics/2019/7/3/20677645/antifa-portland-andy-ngo-proud-boys.

Betz, Joseph. "Violence: Garver's Definition and a Deweyan Correction." *Ethics* 87, no. 4 (1977): 339–351.

Black Protests Vs. White Riots. YouTube video, 2:54. Anonymous Brave New Films, 2015.

Bowden, George. "'Milkshaking': How the Divisive Protest Against Politicians Escalated very Quickly." *HuffPost UK,* May 20, 2019. https://www.huffingtonpost.co.uk/entry/milkshaking-protest-uk_uk_5ce2a731e4b00e035b947b1b.

Bowden, John. "Nigel Farage Briefly Stuck on Brexit Bus Surrounded by Protesters with Milkshakes." *The Hill,* May 22, 2019. https://thehill.com/policy/international/445063-nigel-farage-briefly-stuck-on-brexit-bus-surrounded-by-protesters-with.

Bufacchi, Vittorio. "Two Concepts of Violence." *Political Studies Review* 3, no. 2 (2005): 193–204.

———. *Violence and Social Justice.* London: Palgrave Macmillan, 2007.

Castle, Vicky and Will Rider. "Nigel Farage Stuck on His Brexit Bus because People Turned Up with Milkshake." *Kent Live,* May 22, 2019. https://www.kentlive.news/news/kent-news/nigel-farage-stuck-brexit-bus-2897876.

CDC: Centers for Disease Control and Prevention. "Sexual Violence." https://www.cdc.gov/violenceprevention/sexualviolence/index.html.

Chakelian, Anoosh. ""Lactose Against Intolerance!" how Milkshake Became a Tool of Protest." *New Statesman,* May 16, 2019. https://www.newstatesman.com/politics/uk/2019/05/lactose-against-intolerance-how-milkshake-became-tool-protest.

Cherry, Myisha. "Love, Anger, and Racial Injustice." In *The Routledge Handbook on Love in Philosophy*, edited by Adrienne Martin, 157–168. New York: Routledge, 2019.

Clifton, Derrick. "11 Stunning Images Highlight the Double Standard of Reactions to Riots Like Baltimore." *The Movement,* April 27, 2015. https://mic.com/articles/116680/11-stunning-images-highlight-the-double-standard-of-reactions-to-riots-like-baltimore#.8CvvBczgH.

Conservative Writer Andy Ngo Roughed Up at Portland Antifa/Right Wing Protests. YouTube. The Oregonian, 2019a. https://www.youtube.com/watch?v=8WzMZxT-41k.

Cox, Brendan. *Tweet.* 2019.

Dearden, Lizzie. "Tommy Robinson has Milkshake Thrown Over Him for Second Time in Two Days." *Independent UK,* May 2, 2019. https://www.independent.co.uk/news/uk/crime/tommy-robinson-milkshake-attack-video-warrington-bury-mep-european-elections-a8897156.html.

Elgot, Jessica and Rowena Mason. "Nigel Farage: Migrant Sex Attacks to be 'nuclear Bomb' of EU Referendum." *The Guardian,* June 5, 2016. http://www.theguardian.com/politics/2016/jun/05/nigel-farage-migrant-sex-attacks-to-be-nuclear-bomb-of-eu-referendum.

Garver, Newton. "What Violence Is." In *Philosophy for a New Generation, Second Edition*, edited by A. K. Bierman and James A. Gould, 256–266. New York: MacMillan, 1973.

Giordano, Chiara. "Trump Supporter 'Milkshaked' by Protesters as Tempers Flare Outside Parliament." *Independent UK,* June 4, 2019. https://www.independent.co.uk/news/uk/home-news/trump-supporter-milkshake-video-london-protest-parliament-square-a8943821.html.

Haslanger, Sally. "I—Culture and Critique." *Aristotelian Society Supplementary* 91, no. 1 (2017a): 149–173.

———. "Practical Reason and Social Practices." In *The Routledge Handbook of Practical Reason*, edited by Chang, Ruth and Kurt Sylvan, 68–82. New York: Routledge, 2021.

———. "Racism, Ideology and Social Movements." *Res Philosophica* 94, no. 1 (2017b): 1–22.

————. "What is a Social Practice?" *Royal Institute of Philosophy Supplement* 82 (2018): 231–247.

Hassan, Jennifer. "Milkshake-Wielding Protesters Trap Nigel Farage on His Brexit Bus." *Washington Post,* May 22, 2019. https://www.washingtonpos t.com/world/2019/05/20/what-is-milkshaking-ask-brits-hurling-drinks-right -wing-candidates/.

Iqbal, Nosheen. "'I'm Getting Death Threats,' Says Man Who Threw Milkshake on Tommy Robinson." *The Guardian,* May 5, 2019. http://www .theguardian.com/world/2019/may/05/death-threats-man-threw-milkshake-o ver-tommy-robinson.

Lave, Tamara Rice. "Shoot to Kill: A Critical Look at Stand Your Ground Laws." *University of Miami Law Review* 67 (2013): 827–857.

Lawrence, Doreen, Sayeda Warsi, and Shami Chakrabarti. "Nigel Farage must Apologise for Sex Attack Warning." *The Guardian,* June 6, 2016. https:// www.theguardian.com/politics/2016/jun/06/nigel-farage-must-apologise-for -sex-attack-warning.

Locke, John. *Two Treatises of Government, and; A Letter Concerning Toleration.* New Haven: Yale University Press, 2004.

Lukes, Steven. "Humiliation and the Politics of Identity." *Social Research* 64, no. 1 (Apr 1, 1997): 36–51.

Magra, Iliana. "Why are Milkshakes being Thrown at Right-Wing Politicians Like Nigel Farage?" *New York Times,* May 21, 2019. https://www.nytimes. com/2019/05/21/world/europe/milkshake-nigel-farage.html.

Miller, Ronald B. "Violence, Force and Coercion." In *Violence; Award Winning Essays in the Council for Philosophical Studies Competition*, edited by Jerome A. Shaffer, 9–44. New York: David McKay, 1971.

Nagel, Thomas. *The View from Nowhere.* Oxford: Oxford University Press, 1989.

"Nigel Farage Hit by Milkshake during Newcastle Walkabout." *BBC News,* May 20, 2019b. https://www.bbc.com/news/uk-england-tyne-48339711.

O'Shea, Johnny. "UKIP Candidate Carl Benjamin in Truro Milkshake Melee." *BBC News,* May 10, 2019. https://www.bbc.com/news/uk-england-corn wall-48230438.

Popovic, Srdja and Sophia A. McClennen. *Pranksters Vs. Autocrats: Why Dilemma Actions Advance Nonviolent Activism.* Ithaca: Cornell University Press, 2020.

Richer, Alanna Durkin. "Conviction Upheld for Woman Who Urged Boyfriend's Suicide." *AP News,* February 6, 2019. https://apnews.com/articl e/north-america-us-supreme-court-ma-state-wire-us-news-ap-top-news-abd 449bd66274f698e9ff4d4c2247a8e.

Rodin, David. *War and Self-Defense.* Oxford: Oxford University Press, 2002.

Young, Iris Marion. "Five Faces of Oppression." In *Justice and the Politics of Difference*, edited by Iris Marion Young, 39–65. New Jersey: Princeton University Press, 1990.

Chapter 4

Violence as Persuasive Political Communication

In 2009, the far-right Dutch political party, Nederlandse Volksunie (NVU), organized a series of marches throughout small towns in the Netherlands. Their aim was to publicize their political causes and gain new recruits from around the country.[1] In response, the Dutch antifascist movement enlisted inhabitants of each area to prevent the marches. While Dutch antifa did not explicitly call for violence against the NVU marchers, they titled their strategy *Laat ze niet lopen* (Do not let them walk), and encouraged local immigrants, football hooligans, and members of the traveler community to block the marches by any means necessary.[2] They provided support in the form of legal resources and real-time online updates, which made it possible for local residents to congregate quickly along the NVU march's route in their town.[3]

This strategy was quite effective in shutting down NVU's attempts to broaden its influence. When the NVU marchers tried to make their way through several of the towns, groups of locals threw things at them, and the marchers eventually disbanded. As one antifa activist described it, they responded to the marchers "by chucking everything and anything at them including piles of dogshit in their faces."[4] While mainstream Dutch media outlets decried these actions as violent and illiberal,[5] antifa activists defended the counter-demonstrators. They argued that such minor violence is necessary to hamper extreme right-wing organizing and prevent the need for larger-scale violence down the line.[6] Moreover, as political philosopher Mark Bray explains, antifascists further justify their violence by pointing out that "'rational debate' and the institutions of government have failed to consistently halt the rise of fascism."[7] In contrast, making it difficult or "not worth it" for people to join, or remain members of, far-right political organizations has successfully shut down or seriously hampered these organizations in a number of liberal societies.[8] Indeed, since the well-publicized 2009 "dogshitting" of NVU marchers, its membership has declined, to the extent that it has effectively disappeared from the Dutch political landscape.[9]

Regardless of its social effectiveness, there are some who condemn even such minor instances of militant antifascism as an abandonment of the tenets of liberal political communication. As Aine Donovan, director of the Ethics Institute at Dartmouth, puts it, "Civil society is predicated on civil discourse. This means that we use language, argument and persuasion to make our positions known—not a fist."[10] (Or, we might extrapolate, animal feces.) In response, antifascists reference Henry David Thoreau's 1859 defense of Captain John Brown: "The question is not about the weapon, but the spirit in which you use it."[11] Such antifascists contend that the aim of their actual and threatened violence against far-right political groups is political persuasion. On their view, it gives fascists and would-be fascists "a chance to think about their stance and let[s] them know that it carrie[s] consequences . . . it [gives] them fair warning."[12]

Violence is clearly to be avoided when possible. It tends to threaten autonomy; cause injury, damage, and harm; and violate political and moral rights. When it is oppressive, it prevents groups from full participation in social and political life. The debate over whether to avoid violence in *protest* though, is more often framed in terms of its connection to force. Violence, as we see in the criticism of antifa "dogshitting" NVU marchers, is thought to be conceptually inconsistent with lawbreaking protest in a liberal society understood as a politically communicative act, because it doesn't give the right kinds of reasons. For example, John Rawls writes,

> to engage in violent acts likely to injure and to hurt is incompatible with civil disobedience as a mode of address. Indeed, any interference with the civil liberties of others tends to obscure the civilly disobedient quality of one's act.[13]

Violence does not meet the requirements of public reason. Basically, this requirement is that the rules of a society must be, in some sense, justifiable or acceptable to those they govern. The constraints of public reason give rise, according to Rawls, to a duty of civility. This duty governs communication in the public sphere, which includes acts of protest. Broadly, civility is a moral requirement that when engaged in a public political forum, ordinary citizens make arguments that appeal to their society's shared political values, "avoid appealing to comprehensive (religious and moral) values and listen to others' views with respect and fair-mindedness."[14] When violence is communicative at all, it fails to be civil.[15]

But as N.P. Adams points out, Rawls' constraints on public reason narrow the very concept of civil disobedience to only those cases that would be justified in his near-just society.[16] One, Rawls appeals to his two principles of justice to arrive at these constraints, but other principles, and thus different constraints, are possible in a near-just society. Two, civil disobedience, or, as we prefer to call it, "lawbreaking protest," is meaningful outside of that context. That Rawls' conditions of public reason must obtain for civil disobedience to occur means that even the paradigm cases from which Rawls draws his account—the movements led by King and Gandhi—were not actually instances of the practice.

We want a concept of protest that is suitable for the world in which we actually live, which is not Rawls' near-just society.[17] Rawls' account alerts us to a potential worry for lawbreaking protest: it always pushes the boundaries of public reason. In addition, violent protest in particular may leave the space of public reason altogether. We agree with Adams that the constraints Rawls places on public reason are too narrow to capture protest as a distinct communicative political practice. We contend that in oppressive liberal societies, combating injustice requires going beyond public reasons-giving strictly understood; however, this does not entail that we are no longer doing protest. Indeed, even violent protest may be compatible with engaging in political persuasion.

PROGRESSING TOWARD JUSTICE

Within the context of ideology, Sally Haslanger argues, those fighting for justice will have to engage their interlocutors in activities that are not, in any strict sense, reasons-giving, but instead involve changing the very terms of the debate.[18] They will have to alter their opponents' perceptions, outside of, or in addition to, reasoned argument. This is because the unjust practices that structure our perceptions give us reasons for acting and mask the presence of oppression. For example, if being a good wife involves doing certain household duties, then someone pointing out that the husband could also do those duties, or that there could be a more equitable distribution of household labor and management, is unlikely to be convincing. The wife's reasons for managing the household are given by the practice of being a good wife and, operating within that practice, the reasons for it are largely set aside. Breaking out of those practices, then, is likely to require something that goes beyond reasons-giving. People will need exposure to new practices and new conceptual schemas with their own attendant social meanings to break down their existing ideologies.[19]

In the 1990s, it wasn't uncommon for heterosexuals to inquire of same-sex marriages: "Who is the husband?" or "Who is the wife?" In many cases, this was a deliberate insult, intended to invalidate and mock those relationships, and/or a crude commentary on the sexual practices of same-sex couples. But when raised with genuine incredulity, it could charitably be interpreted as a question about how one would organize a household outside of the traditional gendered roles: How could (would) a gay couple coordinate in response to the demands of a household? Of course, what should have been obvious is that any number of coordination schemas are possible and that gay couples (as well as many straight couples, single people, and non-nuclear family units, for that matter) had already been exploring those alternative arrangements for years. However, without widespread or mainstream exposure to such alternatives, it was easy to see gay marriage, in particular, as at odds with the dominant, heterosexist system of coordination. When the ideological rules of the practice of marriage dictate that each member take on certain (gendered) duties, we can understand the desire to slot married people into the roles of husband and wife.

It may seem like either slotting the partners in gay couples into traditional gender roles, or embracing the use of the new concept of "partners," allowed those in the grip of heterosexist ideology to preserve their practices. In reality, by using traditional titles ("husband" and "husband" or "wife" and "wife"), same-sex couples necessarily contributed to an expanded notion of those concepts. Within the practice of marriage, one could be a husband while performing the duties traditionally assigned to wives, to husbands, or to a combination. Meanwhile, the concept of "partner" found uptake in progressive heterosexual couples looking to redefine their relationship away from traditional gender roles. Conceptualizing one another as partners, with its gender-neutral and business-like tone, not only opened up new possibilities for thinking about how to coordinate the practice of marriage, but also provided a way to talk to and recognize others who were invested in that same redefinition project. Such reconceptualizations are a central tool for those wishing to shift ideology; but they are not reasons-giving. As Haslanger writes, "This disruption [of our concepts] challenges us not by offering reasons, nor by rational discussion, but by queering our language, playing with meanings, and monkey-wrenching or otherwise shifting the material conditions that support our tutored dispositions."[20]

According to Haslanger, these conceptual shifts are part of effective social movements in contexts of ideological infection. Much of this work will be done outside of the eyes of the mainstream, in subcultural spaces where alternative practices are common and creative arrangements are encouraged. Sometimes, protesting for justice will require amplifying these reconceptualizations or employing new conceptual schemas to create new experiences. It is by being encouraged to perceive the world differently that others can come to see what's at issue. While signs, chants, sit-ins, and marches are sending a message, only sometimes is that message best interpreted as either a kind of rational appeal or couched in terms of existing ideology. Other times, it is best interpreted as conveying to the public new conceptual, perceptual, and linguistic tools that allow for new experiences.

The upshot is that communication in protest need not be reasons-giving to be legitimate. In nonideal societies, protesters will have to engage in counter-ideological activities in order to make progress toward justice. How then do we set the outer limits of protest as a practice of persuasive political communication? In other words, what marks the boundary between protest and force? For that, we turn to Adams.

A COMMITMENT TO THE POLITICAL

Following Rawls, Adams understands civil disobedience as a fundamentally communicative act. The civil disobedient aims to draw attention to the tension or inconsistency between their society's political ideals and its current political practices. Moreover, she doesn't simply point out that tension but actively demonstrates it—the civil disobedient breaks the law but is committed to the political ideals. In doing so, she shows how actions on the ground fail to reflect political ideals. This is what gives civil disobedience both its rhetorical force and distinct character as a political practice.[21]

As Adams writes, "The question, then, is how this combination of condemnation and commitment constrains an act of civil disobedience."[22] The condemnation piece is fairly straightforward; the trick is to figure out what civil disobedients must do in order to demonstrate commitment to their society's political ideals, especially given that lawbreaking seems to express disregard for those ideals. "Thus," Adams notes, "much of the debate over the concept of and justificatory conditions on civil disobedience hinges on how the commitment to the political can be expressed."[23]

From here, Adams focuses on contrasting his view that civil disobedience must include a commitment to the political with Rawls' more demanding view that disobedients, to count as such, must demonstrate fidelity to law. Adams' preferred account of this constraint is that it is a commitment to the shared project of living together. He says,

> A commitment to the political presumes the goal—living together—is both communal and long-term. It assumes that we are going to have to work together in the future and so it takes care to preserve relations between us now as well. This takes certain options off the table, namely those options that would render our future cooperation impossible and treats our agonists as outside the political community.[24]

He argues that this is like "Rawls' notion of reasonableness, according to which citizens offer terms of fair cooperation that they are willing to abide by," in the general sense of appealing to others as co-members in a cooperative project, but not in the thicker sense of appealing to a shared sense of justice.[25] Indeed, on this conception of civil disobedience there need not be a shared sense of justice, nor does the cause advocated for have to be a liberal or egalitarian one. One can advocate for illiberal causes in a way that demonstrates a commitment to others as part of the same political project, even if one does not consider them equals.

Preserving a commitment to the shared project of living together is a weaker constraint on protest, and so it is perhaps easier to say what would violate it than what would fulfill it. Lethal violence, for example, is inconsistent with a commitment to the shared project of living together because it removes certain people from the community and so necessarily treats them as outside of a joint political project. However, setting back others' interests, infringing on their rights, and coercing them don't necessarily do so. The question then is whether interpersonal violence always treats others as outside of the political project.

The problem with interpersonal violence, according to Adams, is that it "treats violence as a legitimate decision-making procedure within the community."[26] This is at odds with a commitment to treating others as co-members in a shared political project. Living together is an ongoing practice of offering justifications for decisions. Violence is a way of cutting off that practice of justification, of subjugating others by treating them as mere obstacles to one's will. The use of violence recommends that decisions should be made via subjection to the will of the strongest. In this way, it is fundamentally individualist, rather than a communal project.[27] So, for example, kidnapping an official who is instrumental in administering an unjust policy cannot count as protest, because it treats the official as "outside the bounds of the shared political project" by using physical force to overwhelm her.[28] This, Adams thinks, is the way of militancy rather than civil disobedience.

Adams argues that violence against property does not necessarily suffer from this same problem. While property damage can, in some cases, express a lack of political commitment, such as when one threatens or destroys the resources people need to survive and so pushes them below the level where they can participate as co-members in the community, it need not do so. He concludes, "Since property is not . . . a potential member of the political project of living together, destroying property does not [always] set anyone outside the political project and so does not [necessarily] contradict a commitment to that project."[29] Property damage treats objects as objects, not subjects as objects, and so is compatible with a basic commitment to others, including the property owners, as co-members in a political community. It can be used symbolically to express condemnation—as in the case of protesters burning a police car—without violating a basic commitment to the political. Thus, on Adams' account, civil disobedience can include, conceptually, violence against others' property, but not interpersonal violence.

Adams focuses on the symbolic destruction of property rather than theft as a protest tactic. On the one hand, this is entirely appropriate.

Civil disobedience is a communicative act; it is meant to be expressive, not simply pragmatic. After all, burning a police car is not intended to stop police patrols by taking away their means of patrolling. Were it so intended, then it would be much more effective to burn whole lots of police cruisers. On the other hand, the only example of interpersonal violence Adams discusses—kidnapping an official who is administering an unjust policy—is ambiguous. It could be a symbolic, expressive gesture of condemnation or a practical means of halting the injustice. If it were symbolic, the kidnappers would not demand a policy change in exchange for her safe return. She would be merely "the face of the problem" and so kidnapping her would be a way of drawing attention to the policy. More generally, we can imagine cases of interpersonal violence that are not attempts to subjugate others but are expressions or demonstrations of condemnation. Presumably, Adams' response to such symbolic cases of interpersonal violence would be that they fail to express a commitment to the political. But it is not clear that all interpersonal violence fails in this regard.

INTERPERSONAL VIOLENCE AS MORAL AND POLITICAL SUASION

Think of a woman slapping a man's face who just directed a lewd, inappropriate comment toward her. In Western culture, this form of violence has a particular social meaning. It communicates that she has been insulted and disrespected, and can be used intentionally to express, to both the victim and others, the affront to her dignity. In that way, it is uniquely directed toward the man as a person. Beyond its obvious cruelty, it would make no sense to slap a dog in the face because they keep sniffing your butt. This would communicate nothing to the dog that wouldn't be communicated by a slap anywhere else on its body (viz., that it must stop its current behavior). Moreover, in its canonical form, the face-slap is not an attempt to overpower or suggest that such disputes ought to be resolved through strength. It is an attempt to shock, perhaps, but paradigmatically is used by the physically less powerful who have nothing to gain, and everything to lose, by the suggestion that the will of the strongest ought to prevail. If anything, it is often used in scenarios where the woman fears that such a decision procedure is on the table. The face-slap is not an invitation to further confrontation;

rather, it says to the man, "Stop. Remember that I am a person and you should respect me."

Interpersonal violence that is more clearly politically oriented, rather than privately oriented, can also have this structure. Depending on the context in which it is performed, the ways in which it is controlled, the relative strength of the parties involved, and the particular means of expression, such violence can communicate a clear recognition of the other as a person and a co-member in the shared political project. Thus, it can be protest.

Milkshaking, one could argue, is not a departure from the norms of political discourse, but an attempt to police their boundaries. This minor form of violence signals that certain views fall so far outside the realm of acceptable discourse that they are not worth taking seriously. It is a reminder that espousing such views or engaging in such tactics should be a source of embarrassment, not the grounds of a serious political debate. In targeting Nigel Farage for violence, the milkshakers were not giving up on a project of justification toward those who hold xenophobic or racist attitudes. By embarrassing Farage through covering him in milkshake, they sought to reduce his social status by making him an object of ridicule and not a threat. This is consistent with a view about what has gone wrong in the thought processes of Farage's supporters. They have been seduced by a perception of migrants as dangerous and resources as scarce. Locked inside the echo chamber of social media and right-wing news sources, Farage's fear-mongering and race-baiting have been effective at shaping his followers' perceptions and whipping their anxieties about the future into such a state that they are no longer accurately perceiving either the reality of the situation or the illiberal implications of their position. Humiliating Farage in such a childish way says to his followers, "Don't take him so seriously. He's a clown."

Laughing at someone's views or making fun of their political anxieties might not be the kindest or gentlest approach, but it is not an unfamiliar strategy for trying to break the spell that someone's fear and anxiety have cast over their judgment. Instead, it can indicate recognition of a tendency in all of us to let our fear disrupt our best judgment. The tactic of embarrassment can help others to see the absurdity of their own views and so change their minds. Meanwhile, targeting Farage in particular as a symbol of these views means that the fear that protesters will descend on any gathering of Brexit supporters to douse them with milkshakes is overblown.

The persuasive powers of violent protest are not confined to humiliation. As noted in chapter 2, violent protests might shake up our conceptual schemas and other ideological building blocks which hold in place oppressive practices.[30] For example, throwing bottles and bricks at police invading beleaguered black communities could cause people to question one narrative of police as protectors, and perhaps encourage them to reinterpret the police as occupiers. Returning to Adams' point, the worry with the use of violence is that, even when intended to humiliate or induce conceptual shifts, it will intimidate its targets. Even if violence successfully communicates its message, the attendant intimidation treats its targets as outside the political community, and so such actions fail to be protest.

We disagree that intimidation always treats people as outside of the shared political project. By contrast, in situations of oppression, it may be necessary to remind others in our society that we are engaged in a shared project of living together. Gandhi and King used nonviolence in an attempt to demonstrate their common humanity to their oppressors. Frantz Fanon argues that violence might be effective for asserting oneself as a co-member in political society to the colonial oppressor.[31] Similarly, defending the killing of a slave-catcher by an escaped enslaved person, Frederick Douglass argues that not only was the killing justified but that it was also likely to be helpful in persuading the public that slavery was unjustified.[32] According to Douglass, the public believed that unless one was willing to risk their life for liberty, they had no right to be free. Thus, perceiving enslaved people as docile or accepting of their condition, the public believed them to deserve enslavement. Douglass notes that in killing a slave-catcher rather than submitting to re-enslavement, the kidnapped person provides evidence against this claim.[33]

Furthermore, Douglass argues that the fear and intimidation induced by violence could be a form of prudential and moral suasion. Bernard Boxill, expanding on and defending Douglass' view, argues that fear need not interfere with practical reasons but instead can motivate inquiry into how to avoid that which we fear. Following Hobbes, it is at least partially through fear of the danger that others pose to us that we are convinced to enter into society with them—to seek peace. Fearing that enslaved persons could kill them might motivate slaveholders to extend the basic tenants of morality to enslaved persons, to recognize their co-membership in the political community. These are prudential reasons to accept enslaved persons as members of the slaveholders' political society.

Fear and intimidation can also provide moral suasion that is akin to the kinds of reasons that are acceptable in common notions of liberal protest. In certain circumstances, they appeal to their audiences' political ideals and draw attention to a deep tension between those ideals and their current practices. Slaveholders, Boxill writes,

> were not amoral egoists . . . They were individuals who had internalized the moral principle that human beings have natural rights to life, liberty, and the pursuit of happiness, though of course they suffered from a kind of moral myopia and denied that slaves had these natural rights.[34]

Under these conditions, Boxill argues, the fear induced by enslaved persons' violence could "clear their moral vision."[35] He notes that Douglass came to appreciate that slaveholders already had ample evidence that enslaved persons loved liberty—policies of keeping enslaved persons ignorant and enacting physical cruelty upon them were the necessary strategies for preventing the exercise of that love. Fear, however, could cause the slaveholders to revisit that evidence. The aim, as Boxill reads Douglass, is not to add evidence but to convince the slaveholders to pay attention to that evidence. The slaveholders' pride blinded them to enslaved persons' rights because it caused them to believe their own propaganda—they began to truly believe themselves superior and thereby invulnerable. Attacks by enslaved persons could undermine slaveholders' pride by inducing fear and vulnerability.[36] Fear and intimidation, then, can clear people's vision of false pride and enable them to see what they already believe.

The power of violence to shift and sharpen people's moral vision speaks to the point we made above about the role that non-cognitive features like perception and emotion play in sustaining ideology and through it, widespread oppression. Breaking through those barriers requires activities that, though persuasive, are not strictly speaking reasons-giving. We agree with Adams that lethal violence cannot count as protest; however, some nonlethal violence does treat others as part of the political community and does not recommend the will of the strongest as a decision procedure.

Returning to the activities of antifa activists, the fear and intimidation they produce via violence can be read in at least two ways. On the one hand, throwing animal feces and garbage at neo-Nazis, and fighting them in the streets, might be viewed as an attempt to run the neo-Nazis out of the political community. It might be communicating that neo-Nazis are themselves animals and garbage, and so do not have a place in the shared political project. And certainly, some antifa demonstrators see their activities thusly. They argue that "the antifa goal is to isolate the fascists entirely" and so destroy fascists' ability to achieve any social and political aspirations.[37] On the other hand, such violence might be an attempt to clear proto-fascists' moral vision. It might induce them to remember both their internalized moral commitments and that those who they oppose (e.g., Jewish people, persons of color, immigrants, liberals, socialists, and the LGBTQ+ community) are in reality co-members of their political communities. Some antifa activists see themselves as engaging in such moral suasion—they claim to be trying to bring neo-Nazis back from the brink. As some demonstrators put it, violent antifascism aims to make it not fun to be a Nazi anymore while also shifting the political spectrum so that fascism becomes wholly unacceptable, if not unthinkable.[38] Although violent antifa activism is often derided as militant, this second reading suggests that, in at least some cases, it can be viewed as persuasive and a form of protest.

NOTES

1. Mark Bray, *Antifa: The Anti-Fascist Handbook* (Brooklyn, NY: Melville House, 2017), 200.
2. Bray, *Antifa: The Anti-Fascist Handbook*, 200.
3. Bray, *Antifa: The Anti-Fascist Handbook*, 200.
4. As quoted in Bray, *Antifa: The Anti-Fascist Handbook*, 201.
5. Devin Zane Shaw, *Philosophy of Antifascism: Punching Nazis and Fighting White Supremacy* (London: Rowman & Littlefield Intl, 2020), chapter 1.
6. Bray, *Antifa: The Anti-Fascist Handbook*, 169.
7. Bray, *Antifa: The Anti-Fascist Handbook*, 169.
8. Bray, *Antifa: The Anti-Fascist Handbook*, 174–75.
9. David Art, *Inside the Radical Right: The Development of Anti-Immigrant Parties in Western Europe* (New York: Cambridge University Press, 2011), 78–79.
10. As quoted in Zach Schonfeld, "Is it OK to Punch a Nazi in the Face? Leading Ethicists Weigh in: 'No,'" *Newsweek*, January 24, 2017.

11. As quoted in Shaw, epigraph. Shaw, *Philosophy of Antifascism: Punching Nazis and Fighting White Supremacy.*

12. Bray, *Antifa: The Anti-Fascist Handbook,* 167.

13. John Rawls, *A Theory of Justice, Revised Edition* (Cambridge, MA: Belknap Press, 1999), 321.

14. John Rawls, *Political Liberalism* (New York: Columbia University Press, 1996), 224.

15. As Candice Delmas writes, "Rawls' requirement that civil disobedience be nonviolent implies three intertwined claims: (a) violence coerces, nonviolence persuades; (b) civil disobedience only aims to persuade and as such excludes coercion; and (c) nonviolence is necessary to the communicativeness of civil disobedience." Candice Delmas, "Civil Disobedience," *Philosophical Compass* 11, no. 11 (2016), 683.

16. N. P. Adams, "Uncivil Disobedience: Political Commitment and Violence," *Res Publica* 24 (2018), 479–80.

17. Our argument for this claim is in chapter 1.

18. Sally Haslanger, "Racism, Ideology and Social Movements," *Res Philosophica* 94, no. 1 (2017), 10.

19. Haslanger, "Racism, Ideology and Social Movements," esp. 13–15.

20. Haslanger, "Racism, Ideology and Social Movements," 10.

21. Adams, "Uncivil Disobedience: Political Commitment and Violence," 478.

22. Adams, "Uncivil Disobedience: Political Commitment and Violence," 478.

23. Adams, "Uncivil Disobedience: Political Commitment and Violence," 478.

24. Adams, "Uncivil Disobedience: Political Commitment and Violence," 481.

25. Adams, "Uncivil Disobedience: Political Commitment and Violence," 481.

26. Adams, "Uncivil Disobedience: Political Commitment and Violence," 486.

27. Adams, "Uncivil Disobedience: Political Commitment and Violence," 486.

28. Adams, "Uncivil Disobedience: Political Commitment and Violence," 487. Adams is here discussing a case originally introduced by A. John Simmons.

29. Adams, "Uncivil Disobedience: Political Commitment and Violence," 487–88.

30. Sally Haslanger, from whom we draw our understanding of ideology, does not condone using violence for this purpose. We are departing here from her position.

31. Frantz Fanon, *Black Skin, White Masks,* trans. Richard Philcox (New York: Grove Press, 2008 [1952]), 95.

32. Bernard R. Boxill, "Fear and Shame as Forms of Moral Suasion in the Thought of Frederick Douglass," *Transactions of the Charles S. Peirce Society* 31, no. 4 (1995), 718.

33. Boxill, "Fear and Shame as Forms of Moral Suasion in the Thought of Frederick Douglass," 719.

34. Boxill, "Fear and Shame as Forms of Moral Suasion in the Thought of Frederick Douglass," 727.

35. Boxill, "Fear and Shame as Forms of Moral Suasion in the Thought of Frederick Douglass," 727.

36. Boxill, "Fear and Shame as Forms of Moral Suasion in the Thought of Frederick Douglass," 727–37.

37. Bray, *Antifa: The Anti-Fascist Handbook*, 197. See also his chapter 6 more broadly.

38. Bray, *Antifa: The Anti-Fascist Handbook*, 185–91.

BIBLIOGRAPHY

Adams, N. P. "Uncivil Disobedience: Political Commitment and Violence." *Res Publica* 24, (2018): 475–491.

Art, David. *Inside the Radical Right: The Development of Anti-Immigrant Parties in Western Europe*. New York: Cambridge University Press, 2011.

Boxill, Bernard R. "Fear and Shame as Forms of Moral Suasion in the Thought of Frederick Douglass." *Transactions of the Charles S. Peirce Society* 31, no. 4 (1995): 713–744.

Bray, Mark. *Antifa: The Anti-Fascist Handbook*. Brooklyn, NY: Melville House, 2017.

Delmas, Candice. "Civil Disobedience." *Philosophical Compass* 11, no. 11 (2016): 681–691.

Fanon, Frantz. *Black Skin, White Masks*. Translated by Philcox, Richard. New York: Grove Press, 2008 [1952].

Haslanger, Sally. "Racism, Ideology and Social Movements." *Res Philosophica* 94, no. 1 (2017): 1–22.

Rawls, John. *Political Liberalism*. New York: Columbia University Press, 1996.
———. *A Theory of Justice, Revised Edition*. Cambridge, MA: Belknap Press, 1999.

Schonfeld, Zach. "Is it OK to Punch a Nazi in the Face? Leading Ethicists Weigh in: "No"." *Newsweek,* January 24, 2017. https://www.newsweek.com/richard-spencer-punch-nazi-ethicists-547277.

Shaw, Devin Zane. *Philosophy of Antifascism: Punching Nazis and Fighting White Supremacy*. London: Rowman & Littlefield Intl, 2020.

Chapter 5

Responsibility and Accountability

Permission for Violent Protest

We contend that violent protest is morally justified when (a) the violence is morally permitted defense against an unjust threat to oneself or others and (b) that defensive act is shaped and limited in accordance with the political responsibility to publicly communicate about a perceived injustice.[1] Following Iris Marion Young, we posit a basic political responsibility to speak out and organize with others toward justice. Protest is one means of exercising this responsibility, and it does not, on our view, preclude violence.

In taking up such a political responsibility, we do not thereby disengage from the realm of interpersonal morality, which permits us to defend ourselves and others when we face an unjust threat. Rather, we can (and do) act in both spheres simultaneously. We commit ourselves to the political when we allow this political responsibility to limit and shape our moral permission for defense. Such limitations are more extensive than those included in the constraints that are built into the right of defense. The justification of violent protest does not require that its targets be complicit in the injustice being protested, although they must be accountable for it. So long as defense is justified, violent protest is permitted.

THE POLITICAL RESPONSIBILITY
TO OPPOSE INJUSTICE

Any kind of lawbreaking protest must confront the problem of justification. This problem is most acute in just or nearly just societies in which the general obligation to obey the law is thought to hold. If there is a political obligation to obey the law, how can there be, at the same time, a right or duty to break it? One solution to this problem is to ground the permission to break the law in a natural right or duty to resist injustice or communicate one's moral conscience.[2] This is a strong defense of lawbreaking protest: it holds even in legitimate, democratic regimes and may, in some cases, defend protests even when they advocate injustice. Moreover, by marking out protest as a special kind of lawbreaking, it may come with a set of legal permissions as well. Such theories encourage the legal system to look differently on those who break the law out of moral conscience or perceived injustice.[3]

This kind of solution takes the generally just or nearly just society as a starting point for theorizing. By examining what is possible in that context, theories may arrive at a moral duty or set of permissions that hold even in nonideal societies. More often, however, these theories simply ignore the nonideal, believing it poses no special problems. As Candice Delmas puts it,

> For the most part, theorists do not address what citizens may and ought to do in less-than-nearly-just societies, which fail the test of legitimacy, because they generally believe that disobedience in illegitimate states is not particularly problematic and does not need special justification. In illegitimate states, protestors (and all others) are still bound by natural duties, which constrain their actions, but have no substantive political obligations.[4]

This is not to say that all theorists have ignored the question of justification for lawbreaking protest in nonideal societies. Delmas, in particular, argues for a robust set of political obligations that govern our interactions not only in contexts of legitimate political authority but also in illegitimate, deeply unjust states. These obligations are grounded in the same normative principles (primarily a natural duty to justice) that supposedly underwrite the obligation to obey the law. Here, those normative principles generate an obligation to disobey—to dissent—in ways that are both civil and uncivil, where the latter includes acts that are "covert, evasive, anonymous, violent, or deliberately offensive."[5]

We take a different tack which, though not inconsistent with Delmas', starts in a different place. We begin with the assumption that the world we live in is deeply unjust and that we are all causally implicated in its injustice. We perpetuate it through our daily transactions which tie us to global networks of exploitation and marginalization. Through our everyday interactions, we feed violent systems and further various cultural dominations. At times, these oppressive systems benefit us. At other times, they place us at a disadvantage. At all times, they constrain and limit the options available to us.[6] The networks in which we are caught bind us, seemingly inextricably, to the suffering of others. There is no individual path of escape available. The most conscientious consumer, voter, or community member is faced, even at the best of times, with the choice between doing something bad and doing something worse.

These constraints are best understood as structural. So, when we participate in them (which we cannot help but do) we participate in structural injustice. Feminists, critical race theorists, and social scientists have expended great energy in hashing out the details of social structures, their relationships with both individuals and formal social institutions, and the mechanisms by which they produce and reproduce systems in which individuals occupying certain social positions are left vulnerable to domination and deprivation.[7] We have explored some of this in our discussions of ideology, which is a feature of unjust structures that functions to explain and maintain social inequalities.[8]

For our purposes, the precise details of these oppressive processes are less important than outlining a few basic principles, which we borrow from Young. First, social structures, not individual interactions or formal institutions, are the subject of justice.[9] That said, social structures are not separate from individual interactions. Individuals act and interact within structures like markets, families, and other schemes of mutual cooperation, both formal and informal, which are governed by social rules or norms. As Young writes,

> Depending on the issue, the structural processes that tend to produce injustice for many people do not necessarily refer to a small set of institutions, and they do not exclude everyday habits and chosen actions. Social structures are not a part of the society; instead they involve, or become

visible in, a certain *way of looking* at the whole society, one that sees patterns in relations among people and the positions they occupy relative to one another.[10]

She concludes, "Social structure . . . refers to the accumulated outcomes of the actions of the masses of individuals enacting their own projects, often uncoordinated with many others."[11]

Second, the "point of view" of justice is irreducible to the "point of view" of individual or interpersonal morality.[12] One reason for this is that interpersonal interactions, even when each is morally aboveboard, will tend over time to produce unjust social relations. While individuals can (and will) act badly within institutions, and those morally bad actions are causes for grave concern, in opposing and organizing against injustice we must aim (primarily) at the reform of social structures and only (secondarily or derivatively) at individuals and their actions within those structures.[13]

Third, to claim that injustice has been done is to demand redress and reform. And yet, in situations of structural injustice, Young argues, it is not at all clear who is responsible for addressing oppression.[14] When the solution is complex, demanding fundamental shifts in our most basic institutions and in the very structures that shape the options each of us face, it is not obvious who bears the relevant obligations. Perhaps it is political officials. Certainly, but they face constraints as well on what they can do, assuming that they are inclined to recognize these injustices at all. Fixing structural injustice is not simply a matter of passing laws or appropriating funds, but of creating fundamental changes to our economic and social systems. Who is responsible for making those changes?

We follow Young's social connection model of responsibility in positing that this responsibility is shared by all of us.[15] We are all responsible for reforming the structures in which we live. This forward-looking responsibility is "grounded in the fact that we are all members of a moral community" from which there is no real option of exit.[16] Given the fact of global interconnectedness that now obtains, we cannot remove ourselves from the fray. In virtue of the role we occupy, certain forward-looking duties obtain; so, we are appropriately subject to criticism when we fail to perform them.

Importantly, relying on Robin Zheng's interpretation of Young, on which there are backward-looking, as well as forward-looking, dimensions of responsibility, this responsibility for structural injustice is not justified simply in virtue of occupying a particular role.[17] Our forward-looking responsibility for structural injustice is justified in virtue of our participation in oppression.[18] We are perhaps neither guilty nor liable for the harms we have caused, and yet we are responsible—in the sense that we are accountable—for those harms. As Young claims, "Responsibility from social connection says that those who act within unjust structures have a responsibility to try to make them more just."[19] The reason to engage in resistance is not to keep our hands clean, but because our hands are dirty. In virtue of our dirty hands, we owe each other. And what we owe, importantly, is to come together to work toward justice.[20]

Young's basic contention is that taking up this shared responsibility requires communication. It is a responsibility to speak out, organize, pressure, and convince, but not force. It "is not about doing something by myself . . . but about exhorting others to join me in collective action."[21] For an act to be political, then, it must be public and "aimed at inciting others to join the actors in public opposition."[22] Zheng explains it this way: "As a result of our causal participation in unjust structures, we must take steps to communicate with each other, coordinate our actions, and publicly advocate for structural transformation."[23] This political responsibility is essentially public and communicative, aimed at conveying a message about an ongoing injustice and motivating or convincing others to join in opposing it. It is in this way that we arrive not merely at a permission, but at a political responsibility to protest oppression.

THE NATURE OF THE POLITICAL RESPONSIBILITY TO PROTEST

Protest is not the only means by which one might act on this responsibility to be political. Successful protests will depend on many prior collective efforts, including the creation and maintenance of community organizations, labor unions, advocacy groups, outreach programs, campaigns, and public policy initiatives. Protests themselves are likely to be multipronged: for example, pairing demonstrations with boycotts to increase the pressure for reform. Participation in any of these efforts is a way of taking up political responsibility. Furthermore, some are practically and normatively essential to higher-visibility political activities like public demonstrations.[24]

Our political responsibility can and does consist of many things. However, because it is essentially public and communicative, aims at perceived structural wrongs, and encourages others to join in without the use of force, lawbreaking protest is a paradigmatic instance of taking up the responsibility to be political. At times, lawbreaking protest may be the only option available to exercise this political responsibility.[25] But even when it is not, lawbreaking protest exercises this responsibility by raising awareness, garnering support for the cause, directing sympathetic others to pitch in, and attempting to persuade those who do not yet understand (or agree) to see the merits of the cause.

That it is public and aimed toward collective action means the extension of this responsibility to be political is narrower, and more specific, than the multiplicity of activities that Delmas defends on the grounds of a duty to resist injustice. For example, privately withdrawing one's support for a policy is insufficient.[26] It is only by putting ourselves out there and working with others that we can hope to reform structures. This specific political responsibility makes sense of our duty to protest. We think it further explains why a protest can involve violence. Before discussing violence though, we must explore the distinction between public and private actions.

That this responsibility is essentially public rather than private is a vague condition. As we noted in the previous section, the subject of justice is not so much a particular set of institutions as it is a way of looking at all of the structures in which we are embedded. This means that our individual acts can admit of public and private characters, depending on the point of view that one takes up. So, it is not especially helpful to evaluate the public or private character in terms of some essential feature of an action. Noting where it takes place (e.g., in the home or on the street), the terms it uses (e.g., explicit appeals to a shared conception of justice versus to some moral ideal), and/or the intended audience (e.g., a majority of citizens or a small minority), are all unlikely to yield a definitive ruling on whether the action is properly thought of as public or private.

For example, lawbreaking protest is a paradigmatic expression of political responsibility, but riots are not. Similarly, secretly hacking into a private club and wiping their databases because one disagrees with their discriminatory membership practices may be an effective act of resistance to injustice but, given that it fails to be public or oriented toward collective action, it seems that it is not an expression of one's responsibility to be political. So how then do we know if some act is properly thought of as such an expression? How do we know if someone is *doing politics*? This question is especially important since our project defends violent protest, which is usually thought to go beyond the public sphere.

We can start to answer this question by going back to the point that many of our actions are multimodal; they have both a private (moral) and a public (political) character. Evaluating others' actions as political is a matter of turning a political gaze on those actions. What makes an action an expression of political responsibility depends on there being a kind of outward directedness in the intention of the actor that is attentive to the relevant social meanings and available modes of communication. Its aim is an ever-widening collaborative effort at coordination toward reforming and possibly remaking the structures in which we live. Sometimes, we may find that the political gaze is not the most appropriate for assessing some action, but it is always available. Some acts may be private, aimed at preserving one's own moral character in the face of injustice, but those too can be subject to a political judgment that criticizes them precisely for their failure to be more robustly political. We are never solely in the public political realm or the private moral realm. We are always in both.

Why are you shopping at this grocery store? Perhaps because you have kids at home, and you have a moral responsibility to make sure they are fed. You also have a job that you have to do, in order to have enough money to feed, clothe, and educate those kids. This may mean that the only grocery store you can afford to shop at is this one. You do no wrong, from a private moral perspective, in shopping at this store. However, your shopping at this store does, from a public political perspective, contribute to and perpetuate unjust, oppressive structures. It supports domination, violence, and exploitation. Assessing your actions from this perspective, you are responsible, not in the sense of being liable, but in Young's sense of being accountable.

Protesters' acts are also multimodal in this way—they are both moral and political and so can be evaluated from either perspective. When you protest in the streets, you may be fulfilling your political responsibilities but neglecting your moral ones. These two examples show that there is, as Young notes, a fundamental, inescapable tension between what is demanded of us morally by our interpersonal relationships and what is demanded of us politically by the world.[27] In response to this tension, one can act in one of three ways: resolve it in favor of the demands of interpersonal morality, resolve it in favor of the demands of justice, or try to reduce it by bringing the demands of interpersonal morality into alignment with the political responsibility to justice.

EVALUATING PROTEST FROM A MORAL AND POLITICAL PERSPECTIVE

Protesters, we argue, can take the third path. When the moral realm gives us permission for defense, it need not always be ignored and subsumed by our political responsibilities. One way of reducing this tension is to understand nonviolent protest or civil disobedience (which fulfills the political responsibility) as a kind of long-term defensive strategy (which meets the moral permission). The other, equally reasonable, option is to shape our permission for defense in light of our political responsibility to public communication. Our defensive actions are then used communicatively, expressing our political responsibility as well as our moral permissions.[28]

In the previous chapter, we argued that the conceptual limits of lawbreaking protest are set by a commitment to the political, and that this commitment can include interpersonal violence within its scope. Certainly, one can remain committed to a shared cooperative project of living together while violently defending oneself and others against immediate unjust threats. It is sometimes necessary to do so, to avoid being eliminated from the project. Take, for example, a black female protester captured in a viral video being arrested while protesting by Indianapolis police.[29] She is groped by the officer, to which she responds by shoving her body back into him and twisting out of his grasp. This is an act of self-defense—whether it is justified though, depends on certain conditions discussed below. It is also, we argue, a potential act of protest. In that moment, she publicly condemns the manner in which she is being treated by those she is protesting. She, we think, fulfills her moral permission in a way that works to resolve the tension with her political responsibility. By doing so, she is expressing a commitment to the political.

As we have seen, lawbreaking protest is grounded in a political responsibility. It is a practice of communicating toward collective action to bring about structural change. The limits of the practice of protest do not give us a reason to stop short of interpersonal violence, since it can be communicative. Violence is a manifestation of a distinct kind of justificatory project. It can play with social meanings, undermine concepts, and use humiliation and fear to break down ideological barriers and clear others' moral vision. When violent protest is justified, it uses moral permission to engage in defense to fulfill a political responsibility to communicate toward collective action in order to fight injustice.

This justification depends on establishing whether, and when, individuals have the moral permission to defend themselves and others when they are either considering, or are in the midst of, protest. Traditionally, the right to self- and other-defense is an intuitive corollary of the rights to autonomy and bodily integrity: when there is an active and ongoing illegitimate or unjust threat to these basic human rights, people have a moral permission to defend themselves (and others) against that threat of wrongdoing. This is widely accepted in liberal theory. As Judith Jarvis Thomson writes, "what could be clearer than that morality permits a person to save his or her life against threats to it?"[30] Defense is different than vengeance or punishment; it is a permission to save yourself and others from active and ongoing unjust threats against your basic rights, rather than retribution for a past wrong. This means that the violation, or threatened violation, must be both real—it cannot be simply subjectively perceived[31]—and occurrent.

Contrast fighting for reparations for American slavery with fighting for the cessation of contemporary police brutality. The first cannot be defensive in nature, because it is a response to a historical wronging. The second has the potential to be defensive, because it is a response to an active and ongoing unjust threat against, and violation of, people's basic human rights to bodily integrity and autonomy. When police are present at a protest, they may represent this threat. This example draws out another aspect of defense, which is that it is morally permitted when you have no reasonable expectation that a political authority will protect you. Black Americans, given the history of racist policing in the United States, may reasonably consider the police and other relevant authorities to be threatening and dangerous, rather than protective. So, in protest, it is reasonable for black civilians to read police interactions as unjustly threatening and defend themselves.[32]

Similarly, Rohingya Muslims in Myanmar are morally permitted to defend themselves against Myanmarese security forces. The country's majority Buddhist population does not see the security forces as a threat, because those forces are not threatening them; thus, they often call on the Rohingya to cease their defensive actions, because the majority perceives the Rohingya's actions as aggressive. But this is simply because the Buddhist majority does not understand or believe that the Rohingya face an active and ongoing unjust threat from the country's security forces. Given the Rohingya's actual situation, and their reasonable expectations based on their history and lived experiences, they are morally permitted to defend themselves, and their communities, from the security forces' occurrent unjust threats and violations.

The moral permission to engage in defense in protest is itself limited in certain ways. First, you are only permitted to do what is necessary to stop the unjust violation or threat. To do more than is necessary would be to step over the line from defense to vengeance or punishment. It is incredibly difficult to determine what is necessary to block or stop the occurrent threat or violation in any particular case. In the legal realm, one accepted standard for necessity in defense is reasonableness: if a reasonable person, when faced with the same situation, would regard the defensive action as necessary, then it is deemed to be so. But here we run into the usual issues regarding what constitutes a reasonable person. This is especially problematic in a society with severe and ongoing epistemic oppression, where members of oppressed groups are commonly regarded as unreasonable as a matter of course.[33] So, when attempting to determine whether the particular defensive means used in any particular protest against oppression are necessary, we maintain that the benefit of the doubt should go to the victim rather than the aggressor. This is both because our epistemic biases will tend to sway us incorrectly in the other direction, and because the victims of oppression, having lived with it over time, are more likely to be able to accurately judge what is, and is not, necessary to their and others' defense.[34]

Second, defense must also be proportionate; it must not do excessive damage out of proportion to the relevant good it will do. While proportionality is an inexact standard, Suzanne Uniacke describes it as follows:

Proportionate self-defense requires that the threat fended off/interest protected pass a threshold of comparable seriousness in relation to the harm inflicted on the attacker . . . only harm that exceeds a threshold of comparable seriousness is impermissible because disproportionate.[35]

For instance, Hugo Grotius maintains that a person is entitled to use whatever force is necessary—up to and including lethal force—to ward off an unjust bodily injury. By contrast, David Rodin argues that the use of lethal force to defend against nonlethal, nonpermanent flesh wounds is disproportionate, because the harm inflicted so far exceeds the harm avoided.[36] Questions of comparable seriousness are hard to answer, but there is something to the constraint of proportionality in cases of protest. The degree of defensive harm it is acceptable to inflict on an attacker—what someone may do in defense—depends on the seriousness of the unjust threat that the attacker poses. You may not kill someone to prevent them from engaging in hate speech, even if that were the only way to stop them.

The more serious difficulty with proportionality comes when we must compare wildly different kinds of harms. Is it proportionate to respond to unjust threats to political liberty with bodily harm? Can a person assault a neo-Nazi who tries to intimidate them into leaving the country? It is not only the harms that must be compared and weighed, but also the nature of the wrongful violation that the unjust threat represents.[37] Sometimes rights violations are not particularly harmful (i.e., some cases of paternalistic compulsion do not make the victim worse off), but they are still wrongful and so may be defended against. Judgments of proportionality must take into account that the interest protected via defense is not merely a person's life, liberty, or bodily integrity, but also their rights to these, and more generally, their rights against interference, which may be more or less substantial in particular cases.[38] Given this moral asymmetry, the harm inflicted in defense in protest, to be proportionate, need not be restricted so that it is roughly equivalent to the initial threatened harm (e.g., a bottle for a tear gas canister), but must instead involve a judgment of comparative value between the seriousness of the threatened/occurrent injustice (police brutality) and the damage that the defense will cause (perhaps some physical and psychological injury).

In other words, what a person or group may do in defense depends not only on how harmful the active and ongoing unjust threat is, but also on what's being threatened, both immediately and in the longer term. Consider the amount of ongoing oppression in contemporary liberal societies, as well as its nature. In at least some cases, oppressed groups' lives are being directly and indirectly attacked over time. As Michelle Alexander has convincingly argued, the contemporary American criminal justice system functions, through the mechanisms of mass incarceration based on the "wars" on drugs and crime, to make black Americans a permanent underclass in U.S. society.[39] In addition, these "wars" encourage the invasion of black communities by highly-armed squads of police, which makes violent confrontations and rights violations by police near inevitable, because of both police ideologies and black Americans' accurate perceptions of being subject to active and ongoing unjust threats to their lives, livelihoods, and basic human and political rights.[40] Combine this with the institutional racism also present in the education systems, the political systems, and the private and public business sectors, and what one has is black Americans being degraded and killed by inches.[41] The nature of this structural injustice makes it reasonable for protesters to regard particular unjust threats as both immediately provocative and as contributing to systemic harms and wrongs. Nonlethal violent defense is proportionate when what is at stake, what is being unjustly threatened, is people's lives. In comparison, throwing a milkshake at a politician, chucking a tear gas canister at a heavily armored cop, or hitting a white supremacist with a shoe or a fist, are simply not out of bounds.

It is true that people's ideological blinders sometimes prevent them from seeing this. There is a strong bias against recognizing the slow harms of oppression as being just as weighty, if not more so, as the fast harms that are the result of violent defensive actions. There are undoubtedly many reasons for this cognitive quirk; but it is important not to confuse suddenness with seriousness here. The injustice of oppression, in combination with the fact that it takes years off of people's lives, can together make it the case that nonlethal defense in response to provocative actions is proportionate, as well as necessary. However, concerns about proportionality give some reason to avoid engaging in lethal defense, if at all possible. While lethal defense can be proportionate, as well as necessary, it is such a significant, and final, harm that it is difficult to say what threatened unjust injury is of comparable seriousness.[42] This gives us reason to maintain that the moral permission to engage in defense stops short, in most (but not all) cases, of permitting lethal defensive violence.

In addition to being both necessary and proportionate, some theorists argue that defense must have a reasonable chance of success. The suggested constraint is not that defense, to be justified, will *obviously* or *very likely* succeed. Rather, the claim is that it must be reasonable to think that there is a more-than-minimal chance that the defense will have the outcome of blocking, preventing, or ameliorating the occurrent unjust threat or violation. When defense is futile, it is not justified. As Edmund Flanigan puts the point, in some cases, the moral permission to engage in defense is outweighed by prudential concerns. This is especially true, he contends, when the prudential considerations stem from "the predictable further conduct of one's very same aggressor."[43] When attempted defense will predictably lead to further, more egregious harms with no hope of recourse, it's better not to engage in defense in the first place.

This is the nature of "The Talk" that black Americans have with their children. An essential element of The Talk is being very clear that any attempt to defend yourself against the agents of the state will inevitably bring further state aggression down, not only on you, but also on your family and community. If you try to fight the police, they will kill you, harass your family, and invade and terrorize your community, all with impunity. So be polite, keep your hands visible, and above all, do not try to defend yourself no matter what, as that will inevitably be read as aggression and have the consequences just listed, among others.[44] As Flanigan notes, the point illustrated by The Talk is that in many modern states, individual resistance against unjust state-authorized force is futile; it will inevitably lead only to more harms and wrongs, given both the nature and the power of those states.[45]

> "The Talk" is obviously not advice about the right way to interact, morally, with agents of the state; nor is it about the moral permissions of subjects and limits of rightful state action. It is advice about how not to get hurt, which is to say advice about prudence.[46]

Such prudential concerns arise often in discussions of violent protest. People claim that violent protest is prohibited, not because it is morally wrong (sometimes, they allow that it is morally permitted!), but because it does not work. The general move here seems to be something like the following: exercises that are essentially ineffectual are not justified, even when there is an apparent moral permission to engage in them, because justification is ultimately tied up with consequences—with what will or is likely to occur—as well as with what people do. While we agree that consequences must be considered when determining what course of action to take, we nevertheless disagree with Flanigan's strong claim that prudential concerns can sometimes be powerful enough to wholly outweigh the moral permission to engage in defense.[47]

First, it is not clear that defense, even when it does not succeed (wholly or in part) in preventing the unjust threat or violation, is essentially ineffective. Consider the case of Polish Jewish ballerina Franceska Mann, who was brought to Auschwitz-Birkenau extermination camp in 1943. Upon being led to the antechamber of the gas chambers with a group of other women and ordered to strip, she danced distractingly and managed to grab an SS officer's gun, killing him and three other guards before being murdered.[48] Her defensive acts were imprudent, certainly, but were they wholly ineffectual? Arguably, her actions gave hope to her fellow prisoners and stiffened their resolve, and, at the very least, made it so there were four fewer Nazis engaged in atrocities.[49] Four fewer genocidaires does not stop the injustice, but it is not nothing, and to say that it is misunderstands both the short- and long-term social and political consequences of defense. Defense not only attempts to protect against the immediate threatened harm, but can also have a transformative psychological effect on both those who engage in it and those who witness it.[50]

Furthermore, speaking directly about violent protest, it is not clear that violent protest does not work. As we argued in chapter 2, violent protest is sometimes successful, in the sense that it is causally linked to subsequent social and political changes that prevent or ameliorate the relevant injustices. Although Erica Chenoweth and Maria J. Stephan argue against this prudential point,[51] they in places seem to lump all violence together in a way that does not distinguish between lethal violence, armed resistance, and nonlethal acts of defense and resistance. As Mark Bray and others note, once you make these distinctions, the conclusions that Chenoweth and Stephan try to draw about the ineffectiveness of violence in protest become less obvious.[52] What it means, then, for some defensive act to have a reasonable chance of success is more complicated than Flanigan perhaps allows.

Second, we could instead read Flanigan as pushing not a prudential concern, but a moral concern about the downstream consequences of engaging in defense. When engaging in defense will reliably hurt those that you love and care about, as well as your broader community, you should not do it, even when you have the requisite moral permission. Michael Walzer notes that the crime of serious unjust aggression is that it forces people to choose between their (and others') lives and their most basic rights.[53] In such situations, Walzer contends, "they are always justified in fighting; and in most cases, given that harsh choice, fighting is the morally preferred response."[54]

Walzer rejects appeasement as a response to the prudential concerns often associated with engaging in defense because "even when [appeasement] is the better part of wisdom, [it] diminishes [our common] values and leaves us all impoverished."[55] By contrast, engaging in defense vindicates our commitment to certain values; it confirms and enhances our desire to live in a world where all people are treated with dignity, where their rights are respected, and they are able to "freely shape their separate destinies."[56] But that kind of society, and world, "is never fully realized; it is never safe; it must always be defended."[57] Walzer's point is that the great importance we attach to the values that are under attack when state-authorized injustices go unopposed necessitates defense, even when we think such defense is likely to fail.[58] Part of what we do when we fight back is fight for the moral character of the world in which we want to live. That commitment is not reducible to calculations about what is likely to occur.

Walzer concedes that justice and prudence sit in uneasy relation to one another, and so the decision to defend must be made, in the first instance, by the people who will have to endure what follows.[59] It is not up to us to tell a black protester groped by the police to defend herself from police brutality; that is a decision best made by her and her fellows. What we can say is that her decision to engage in defense should be met with solidarity and support, rather than prudentially-based fear, derision, or victim-blaming. We cannot be sure what it would mean to "correctly" or "rightly" weigh justice against prudence. Thus, we are left with ensuring that such decisions are made by the right people and groups, namely, those who are directly affected.

The final traditional constraint on the moral permission to engage in defense is that those targeted in defense must be *liable* for the threatened unjust harm or violation. For defensive actions to be permissible, the person targeted must have lost their standing to claim that they should not be harmed by others.[60] Usually, such standing is lost by being morally responsible for, or having responsible control over, the threatened or ongoing injustices or violations to which the defensive actions are a response. For instance, if you wrongfully threaten to cut someone with a knife, you lose standing to claim that they not harm you in defense. When such standing is lost in this way, we say that you are *liable for* the wrongful threat, and so are *liable to* defensive harm, whether it is at their hands or done on their behalf. Although there is serious controversy surrounding how to draw the lines of liability,[61] this baseline understanding makes clear the intuitive link between a person's liability to defensive harm and their responsibility for, or control over, their occurrent wrongful acts.

This leads immediately to a problem: It is not clear who is responsible for, or has the relevant control over, the occurrent injustices that oppressed groups face in contemporary liberal societies. Structural oppression is a feature of societies, rather than individuals: Who then may be defensively targeted in response to occurrent unjust threats and violations? Initially, we can say that those who are immediately doing the unjust threatening and violating—that is, police in the midst of attacking peaceful protesters—may be targeted in defense, as they do have control over their particular actions in the relevant sense. A police officer dressed in riot gear advancing menacingly on unarmed protesters is not like an automaton or a man stuffed into a barrel which is about to crush you (to borrow Robert Nozick's case of an immediate threat who is obviously not responsible for, or in control of, the unjust threat he poses).[62] Rather, the police officer who is an immediate threat does have the relevant kind of control—he could choose to act otherwise (e.g., to not behave menacingly, to not hit or kettle protesters, or to not shoot tear gas canisters into crowds) in those particular circumstances. To deny this is, as we argued in chapter 2, to fail to recognize that police officers are persons who can and do make (sometimes difficult) choices about their specific actions in context. Such immediately threatening police are liable to defensive attack in the traditional sense.

However, the question of who may be targeted in defense becomes more complicated when we move away from the clear-cut cases of liable unjust threats. Consider police who are simply standing, ostensibly fulfilling their traditional role at protests (protecting protesters and others, maintaining calm, etc.). Given the background oppressive conditions of some societies, it is reasonable for protesters to read such police as an unjust threat. However, these police may not be liable, or liable enough, to be appropriately defensively targeted on such grounds.[63]

Following Young though, we maintain that even when people are not liable, they are still *accountable* for the structural injustices facing black Americans, and this licenses certain defensive responses.[64] Because police at the protest are reasonably read as posing an unjust threat and are accountable, they may be targeted in defense. However, because accountability grounds particular forward-looking political responsibilities, the defense that is ethically permitted must be politically shaped to be justified. The specific defensive actions must have a political valence, namely, they must be readable as efforts to communicate about a serious injustice in the hopes of instigating collective action toward change.[65]

When otherwise permissible defensive actions are constrained and shaped in this political way, defense is also protest.[66] Given its communicative qualities, this subset of defensive actions may include violence.[67] On this reading, throwing bottles and bricks at police during protests against police brutality, milkshakes at politicians who are engaged in hate speech, and dog feces at white supremacists marching in the streets, can be both defense *and* protest. They are potentially necessary, proportionate, arguably prudent actions that take aim at those who are currently posing an unjust threat in a way that publicly communicates toward collective action for political change. The tension between the moral and the political can thus be resolved by doing two things at the same time, via the exact same actions.

The vindication of our theory about the permissibility of violent protest does not rest on whether or not people are always right about their moral permissions for defense. For example, there are protesters who think that they act in other-defense when they blow up abortion clinics, or target and injure doctors and nurses to save fetuses and communicate a powerful condemnation of the practice of abortion. Even if they shape such attacks to avoid lethality, they are wrong to target these personnel. An early-term fetus is not a person and protection of such fetuses is not an act of other-defense.[68]

Nor does our theory depend on would-be protesters consistently shaping their defensive actions in protests with an eye toward their political responsibilities. Individuals may become carried away by the passion of their convictions, ignoring both whether they in fact have permission for self-and-other defense and whether they are actively shaping that permission so that their defensive actions are protest. In 2016, a group of protesters led by Ammon Bundy occupied a wildlife refuge in Oregon to protest federal government management of public lands like the one they occupied. Whether or not they are right that the restrictions placed on ranchers by the federal government is unjust, their unlawful occupation was an exercise of their political responsibility to speak out against a perceived structural injustice. Given the nature of their protest, the fact that at least one protester, LaVoy Finicum, chose to evade federal authorities in a high-speed chase rather than surrender might be reasonably understood as an act of self-defense shaped by his political responsibilities. However, when he was stopped by police, exited the vehicle, and reached for a firearm, signaling the threat of lethal violence rather than the desire to publicly communicate, his protest ended. He moved into the realm of revolutionary violence.[69]

To sum up, violent protest is permitted, and perhaps justified, when the protesters can reasonably read their targets as posing an unjust immediate and/or serious threat, and those targets are accountable.[70] These factors license defensive responses—the range of those responses is constrained not only by necessity, proportionality, and prudence, but also by the targets' accountability, which authorizes communicative responses geared toward critique and reminder, rather than blame, guilt, or punishment. Given our account of violence, these constraints do not rule out violent responses. When activists act in accordance with these constraints, and shape their responses so that they are in line with their own political responsibility to communicate toward collective action against injustice, they are protesters who have resolved the tension between the demands of immediacy and justice.

NOTES

1. It may also be justified in other circumstances. For example, Edmund Tweedy Flanigan writes that violence is morally permissible as protest "when it is a fitting response to those circumstances." Edmund Tweedy Flanigan, "From Self-Defense to Violent Protest," *Critical Review of International Social and Political Philosophy* (2021), 1.

2. See Ronald Dworkin and Kimberley Brownlee for examples of these kinds of arguments. Ronald Dworkin, *Taking Rights Seriously* (Cambridge, MA: Harvard University Press, 1977); Kimberley Brownlee, *Conscience and Conviction: The Case for Civil Disobedience* (Oxford: Oxford University

Press, 2012). For more traditional liberal arguments supporting lawbreaking protest, see chapter 1.

3. For examples of how the legal system might accommodate such lawbreaking protests, see again Dworkin and Brownlee. Dworkin, *Taking Rights Seriously*; Brownlee, *Conscience and Conviction: The Case for Civil Disobedience.*

4. Candice Delmas, *A Duty to Resist: When Disobedience should be Uncivil* (New York, NY: Oxford University Press, 2018), 9.

5. Delmas, *A Duty to Resist: When Disobedience should be Uncivil*, 17.

6. Iris Marion Young, *Responsibility for Justice* (Oxford: Oxford University Press, 2011), 56.

7. For a good summation of these discussions, see Alexis Shotwell, *Against Purity: Living Ethically in Compromised Times* (Minnesota: University of Minnesota Press, 2016).

8. Our discussions of ideology can be found in chapters 3 and 4.

9. Iris Marion Young, "Political Responsibility and Structural Injustice," The Lindley Lecture, University of Kansas (2003), 1–21; Young, *Responsibility for Justice*, chapter 2.

10. Young, *Responsibility for Justice*, 70.

11. Young, *Responsibility for Justice*, 62.

12. Young, *Responsibility for Justice*, 70–71.

13. Young, *Responsibility for Justice*, esp. chapters 3 and 4.

14. Young, *Responsibility for Justice*, chapter 4, esp. 95–104.

15. Young, *Responsibility for Justice*, 110.

16. Robin Zheng, "What Kind of Responsibility do we have for Fighting Injustice? A Moral-Theoretic Perspective on the Social Connections Model," *Critical Horizons* 20, no. 2 (2019), 116, 122.

17. Zheng, "What Kind of Responsibility do we have for Fighting Injustice? A Moral-Theoretic Perspective on the Social Connections Model," 118.

18. Zheng, "What Kind of Responsibility do we have for Fighting Injustice? A Moral-Theoretic Perspective on the Social Connections Model," 118.

19. Young, *Responsibility for Justice*, 180.

20. Zheng, "What Kind of Responsibility do we have for Fighting Injustice? A Moral-Theoretic Perspective on the Social Connections Model," 112; Young, *Responsibility for Justice*, 92.

21. Young, *Responsibility for Justice*, 93.

22. Young, *Responsibility for Justice*, 90.

23. Zheng, "What Kind of Responsibility do we have for Fighting Injustice? A Moral-Theoretic Perspective on the Social Connections Model," 117.

24. We return to this point in chapter 6.

25. In discussing Hannah Arendt's work on political responsibility, on whom she draws, Young mentions that Arendt gives only one example of Germans who took up a political (as opposed to a private moral) responsibility

against the Nazi regime. Young, *Responsibility for Justice*, 90. The Scholl siblings, students at the University of Munich, were executed for treason for distributing leaflets criticizing the Nazi government and enjoining the population to rise up against it. In defense of her actions, Sophie Scholl is reported as saying, "Somebody, after all, had to make a start. What we wrote and said is also believed by many others. They just don't dare express themselves as we did." John Simkin, "Sophie Scholl," Spartacus Educational, 2016.

26. As Zheng helpfully puts the distinction, "responsibility in the political sense concerns the relationship between the individual and *others*, as a matter of politics: did she *publicly* resist, and did she attempt to change the social circumstances that generate such wrongs? . . . Young contrasts Italian vs. Danish resistance: although the Italians deferred, undermined, and refused to carry out Nazi directives, they did not *publicly* denounce them as did the Danish, rendering their resistance moral rather than political. The difference between these two types of responsibility, then, lies in whether actions are aimed at bringing about change in the world rather than merely preserving one's character." Zheng, "What Kind of Responsibility do we have for Fighting Injustice? A Moral-Theoretic Perspective on the Social Connections Model," 110.

27. Young, *Responsibility for Justice*, 165.

28. This is different from an appeal of last resort, where having tried and failed to persuade others to pay attention to and oppose some injustice, one finally resorts to defense. Though lawbreaking protest is usually not the first tool to reach for in opposing injustice, our view does not morally require that protesters exhaust other communicative options before turning to the use of violence. Violence is available as a potentially justified protest tactic whenever the basic conditions of a political responsibility to oppose injustice and a moral permission for defense are met. Its actual justification will depend on process-related normative constraints, like an analysis of the communicative context. See chapter 6 for more details.

29. Greg T. Doucette, *Tweet* (2020).

30. Judith Jarvis Thomson, "Self-Defense," *Philosophy & Public Affairs* 20, no. 4 (1991), 283.

31. People can be seriously mistaken about whether their basic rights are under threat. For defense to be justified, it must be reasonable for someone to think that there is an actual illegitimate threat of wrongdoing, or an active and ongoing violation of a person's or group's basic human rights. We discuss what makes such readings reasonable throughout the remainder of the chapter.

32. This permission is not necessarily limited to black Americans in police protest; but it is an instructive case.

33. For more on epistemic oppression, see chapter 1.

34. It is *possible* that people under oppression will take unnecessarily harsh measures in defense of themselves or others, but unlikely; more often than not

they do the minimum necessary, but are misjudged by a broader society that does not understand the nature and severity of the occurrent injustices they face. Claudia Card, "Questions regarding a War on Terrorism," *Hypatia* 18, no. 1 (2003), 164–69.

35. Suzanne Uniacke, "Proportionality and Self-Defense," *Law and Philosophy* 30, no. 3 (2011), 256.

36. David Rodin, *War and Self-Defense* (Oxford: Oxford University Press, 2002), 48–49.

37. Uniacke, "Proportionality and Self-Defense," 261–62.

38. Uniacke, "Proportionality and Self-Defense," 261–62.

39. Michelle Alexander, *The New Jim Crow: Mass Incarceration in the Age of Colorblindness* (New York: The New Press, 2012).

40. It is no surprise that poor black neighborhoods in the United States are often depicted as "war zones." What is incorrect about such coverage is the implicit—and sometimes explicit—claim that the police are on the side of justice. They are often the unjust aggressors in such situations. See chapter 2 for more discussion of this point.

41. For documentation of the institutional racism within these systems, see, among others, Derrick Darby and John L. Rury, *The Color of Mind: Why the Origins of the Achievement Gap Matter for Justice* (Illinois: University of Chicago Press, 2018); Jennifer Kling and Leland Harper, "The Semantic Foundations of White Fragility and the Consequences for Justice," *Res Philosophica* 97, no. 2 (2020), 325–44.

42. Surely some threatened unjust injuries are of comparable seriousness; otherwise, war and lethal self-defense would always be impermissible. Following liberal accounts of just war theory, we do not accept those claims. However, like many contemporary just war theorists, we err on the side of caution and so contend that proportionality blocks the use of lethal defensive violence in all but the most obvious and clear-cut of cases.

43. Flanigan, "From Self-Defense to Violent Protest," 9.

44. This description of The Talk was provided in informal conversation with black Americans who wish to remain anonymous. It is also outlined in Flanigan, "From Self-Defense to Violent Protest," 5.

45. Flanigan, "From Self-Defense to Violent Protest," 4–5.

46. Flanigan, "From Self-Defense to Violent Protest," 5.

47. Flanigan, "From Self-Defense to Violent Protest," 9.

48. Gideon Graif, *We Wept without Tears: Testimonies of the Jewish Sonderkommando from Auschwitz* (New Haven, CT: Yale University Press, 2005), 359.

49. Filip Müller, *Eyewitness Auschwitz: Three Years in the Gas Chambers* (New York: Stein and Day, 1979), 146.

50. Frantz Fanon, *The Wretched of the Earth*, 1st Evergreen ed. (New York: Grove Weidenfeld, 1991), 51.

51. Erica Chenoweth and Maria J. Stephan, *Why Civil Resistance Works: The Strategic Logic of Nonviolent Conflict* (New York: Columbia University Press, 2011).

52. Mark Bray, *Antifa: The Anti-Fascist Handbook* (Brooklyn, NY: Melville House, 2017), 179–85; Mohammad Ali Kadivar and Neil Ketchley, "Sticks, Stones, and Molotov Cocktails: Unarmed Collective Violence and Democratization," *Socius: Sociological Research for a Dynamic World* 4 (2018), 1–16.

53. Michael Walzer, *Just and Unjust Wars: A Moral Argument with Historical Illustrations, Fourth Edition* (New York: Basic Books, 1977), 51.

54. Walzer, *Just and Unjust Wars: A Moral Argument with Historical Illustrations, Fourth Edition*, 51.

55. Walzer, *Just and Unjust Wars: A Moral Argument with Historical Illustrations, Fourth Edition*, 71.

56. Walzer, *Just and Unjust Wars: A Moral Argument with Historical Illustrations, Fourth Edition*, 72.

57. Walzer, *Just and Unjust Wars: A Moral Argument with Historical Illustrations, Fourth Edition*, 72.

58. Of course, as Walzer points out, those under attack should not have to defend themselves alone; others should come to their defense and aid. Walzer, *Just and Unjust Wars: A Moral Argument with Historical Illustrations, Fourth Edition*, 52.

59. Walzer, *Just and Unjust Wars: A Moral Argument with Historical Illustrations, Fourth Edition*, 71, note 1.

60. That people in general have a claim to not be harmed or wronged by others, unless they act in such a way so as to lose that standing, is a basic premise of rights theory, and so we do not defend it here.

61. See, among others, Jeff McMahan, *Killing in War* (Oxford: Oxford University Press, 2009); Jeff McMahan, "The Limits of Self-Defense," in *The Ethics of Self-Defense*, eds. Christian Coons and Michael Weber (Oxford: Oxford University Press, 2016), 185–210; Helen Frowe, *Defensive Killing: An Essay on War and Self-Defence* (Oxford: Oxford University Press, 2014), esp. chapter 4; Jonathan Quong, "Liability to Defensive Harm," *Philosophy & Public Affairs* 40, no. 1 (2012), 45–77.

62. Robert Nozick, *Anarchy, State, and Utopia* (Oxford: Basil Blackwell, 1974), 34–35.

63. Flanigan, "From Self-Defense to Violent Protest," 8.

64. Of course, such defensive responses are still subject to the other constraints on defense that we have already mentioned, including necessity, proportionality, and prudence.

65. Taking defensive actions that are noncommunicative is not ruled out on our account. The political responsibility to publicly communicate does not require people to risk their lives or the lives of others. In defending themselves

and others against attack, a move away from protest, toward militancy, is open to them. But the mere use of violence does not commit them or the character of their actions to militancy.

66. N.P. Adams restricts his focus to constitutive violence—that is, "violence that constitutes the act of civil disobedience: violence in the very act of breaking the law." N. P. Adams, "Uncivil Disobedience: Political Commitment and Violence," *Res Publica* 24 (2018), 483. On his view, related acts of violence do not make the disobedient act violent. Related violence is when the act of disobedience is not itself violent, but the lawbreaking protesters nevertheless engage in some violence like resisting arrest or responding to attacks. Such related violence, Adams argues, is distinct from violent civil disobedience. While we agree with Adams that related violence does not necessarily make an act of protest violent, confining those acts to a separate category means he fails to consider whether defensive violence could also constitute an act or part of an act of lawbreaking protest. For example, a violent response to law enforcement could be used to send or enhance the central message of a protest. The other obvious example, which we introduce in this chapter, is resisting arrest.

67. For a discussion of violence's communicative qualities, see chapter 4.

68. While we have argued that, in the face of skepticism about our current ability to instantiate anything like public reason, we should avoid ruling out some communicative projects (chapter 1), this does not mean that a progressive liberal project can make no determinations and must admit all comers to the negotiating table.

69. For more on this distinction, see chapter 7.

70. Of course, those targets can be liable as well. If so, there is a straightforward moral permission to engage in defense against them. For such defense to be protest, the activists must constrain their defense even against those targets so that it is publicly communicative.

BIBLIOGRAPHY

Adams, N. P. "Uncivil Disobedience: Political Commitment and Violence." *Res Publica* 24, (2018): 475–491.

Alexander, Michelle. *The New Jim Crow: Mass Incarceration in the Age of Colorblindness*. New York: The New Press, 2012.

Bray, Mark. *Antifa: The Anti-Fascist Handbook*. Brooklyn, NY: Melville House, 2017.

Brownlee, Kimberley. *Conscience and Conviction: The Case for Civil Disobedience*. Oxford: Oxford University Press, 2012.

Card, Claudia. "Questions regarding a War on Terrorism." *Hypatia* 18, no. 1 (2003): 164–169.

Chenoweth, Erica and Maria J. Stephan. *Why Civil Resistance Works: The Strategic Logic of Nonviolent Conflict.* New York: Columbia University Press, 2011.

Darby, Derrick and John L. Rury. *The Color of Mind: Why the Origins of the Achievement Gap Matter for Justice.* Illinois: University of Chicago Press, 2018.

Delmas, Candice. *A Duty to Resist: When Disobedience should be Uncivil.* New York, NY: Oxford University Press, 2018.

Doucette, Greg T. *Tweet.* 2020.

Dworkin, Ronald. *Taking Rights Seriously.* Cambridge, Mass: Harvard University Press, 1977.

Fanon, Frantz. *The Wretched of the Earth.* 1st Evergreen ed. New York: Grove Weidenfeld, 1991.

Flanigan, Edmund Tweedy. "From Self-Defense to Violent Protest." *Critical Review of International Social and Political Philosophy* (2021): 1–25.

Frowe, Helen. *Defensive Killing: An Essay on War and Self-Defence.* Oxford: Oxford University Press, 2014.

Graif, Gideon. *We Wept without Tears: Testimonies of the Jewish Sonderkommando from Auschwitz.* New Haven, CT: Yale University Press, 2005.

Kadivar, Mohammad Ali and Neil Ketchley. "Sticks, Stones, and Molotov Cocktails: Unarmed Collective Violence and Democratization." *Socius: Sociological Research for a Dynamic World* 4 (2018): 1–16.

Kling, Jennifer and Leland Harper. "The Semantic Foundations of White Fragility and the Consequences for Justice." *Res Philosophica* 97, no. 2 (2020): 325–344.

McMahan, Jeff. *Killing in War.* Oxford: Oxford University Press, 2009.

———. "The Limits of Self-Defense." In *The Ethics of Self-Defense,* edited by Christian Coons and Michael Weber, 185–210. Oxford: Oxford University Press, 2016.

Müller, Filip. *Eyewitness Auschwitz: Three Years in the Gas Chambers.* New York: Stein and Day, 1979.

Nozick, Robert. *Anarchy, State, and Utopia.* Oxford: Basil Blackwell, 1974.

Quong, Jonathan. "Liability to Defensive Harm." *Philosophy & Public Affairs* 40, no. 1 (2012): 45–77.

Rodin, David. *War and Self-Defense.* Oxford: Oxford University Press, 2002.

Shotwell, Alexis. *Against Purity: Living Ethically in Compromised Times.* Minnesota: University of Minnesota Press, 2016.

Simkin, John. "Sophie Scholl." Spartacus Educational (2016).

Thomson, Judith Jarvis. "Self-Defense." *Philosophy & Public Affairs* 20, no. 4 (1991): 283–310.

Uniacke, Suzanne. "Proportionality and Self-Defense." *Law and Philosophy* 30, no. 3 (2011): 253–272.

Walzer, Michael. *Just and Unjust Wars: A Moral Argument with Historical Illustrations, Fourth Edition*. New York: Basic Books, 1977.

Young, Iris Marion. "Political Responsibility and Structural Injustice." The Lindley Lecture, University of Kansas (2003): 1–21.

———. *Responsibility for Justice*. Oxford: Oxford University Press, 2011.

Zheng, Robin. "What Kind of Responsibility do we have for Fighting Injustice? A Moral-Theoretic Perspective on the Social Connections Model." *Critical Horizons* 20, no. 2 (2019): 109–126.

Chapter 6

Attitudes and Actions

The Responsibilities of Protesters

In Hong Kong, 2019–2020 was marked by protests, violent and nonviolent. The protests were sparked by a proposed extradition bill, the controversial provisions of which would have allowed Hong Kongers to be tried and punished in mainland China. Opponents of the bill argued that it would further erode Hong Kong's increasingly fragile autonomy and the civil liberties of its residents. The aggressive and increasingly violent policing of the initially peaceful demonstrations was a vivid depiction and potential harbinger of the restrictions on liberty which activists continue to fear will accompany full political integration with China in 2047.[1] One protest tactic was to take to the streets in frequent, large-scale illegal demonstrations which inevitably resulted in clashes with police, who showed up to shut them down with tear gas and water cannons laced with a skin-burning chemical. Rather than disperse, protesters defended themselves, wielding umbrella shields and wearing gas masks. They threw Molotov cocktails and bricks, and destroyed property to build barriers that slowed down police advances. Each time, protesters were eventually forced off the streets, but returned week after week. The communicative prospects of these defensive tactics were captured in the following excerpt from an interview on *This American Life* between the show's host, Ira Glass, and a Hong Kong protester, referred to as "Jennifer."

Ira Glass: But I don't understand. So the police want us out of there. They push, they fire tear gas. They spray blue water on everybody. We move back. And then we stand here. And what's our goal?

Jennifer: This has been a very frequently asked question. Nowadays, we're just trying to stand on our own ground, not to be dispersed that easily.
Ira Glass: That's it. Just, the goal is to just stay out as long as you can.
Jennifer: Yeah.
Ira Glass: And then, eventually, the police will push you off the street? So in other words, it's exactly like the entire protest movement leading to 2047. Just try to slow them down as much as you can.
Jennifer: Yes.
Ira Glass: In the end, China will win. But for as long as you can, you'll just stand here in the street.[2]

Whether the audience is other Hong Kongers, mainland China and the Beijing government, the police, or simply their fellow protesters, the communicative content of the protests appears to be similar—there are values at stake that are worth holding onto for as long as possible, even in the face of inevitable defeat.[3] In the case of Hong Kong, exactly which values those are is not always clear. Are the protesters fighting for democracy? Are they defending rights that they fear are being, and will be further, eroded under Chinese rule? Or, are their concerns about cultural preservation in the face of increasing immigration from mainland China?

There are many who disagree with Hong Kong protesters' tactics and/or who do not understand their message. Jennifer and her friend, Tiffany, explain that their parents strongly object to their participation in the protests:

Tiffany: I mean, for my parents, they—we really have some very serious fights.
Ira Glass: And they think, we'll just let China take over Hong Kong, it'll be fine?
Tiffany: I think with our parents, some of the older generation just don't believe, or they are not brave enough to open up their eyes and see what is actually going to happen. They just feel like they did not do anything wrong. As long as you did not do anything wrong, then you'll be fine.[4]

An interview with their parents would likely yield a different assessment of the situation. Their parents might argue that by resolving the tension between their moral permissions and political responsibility in this way—by using violence as a communicative tactic—the protesters are acting manipulatively to create circumstances in which defense is

justified. While they may have a moral permission to defend themselves, protesters' active participation in violent confrontations makes
them partially liable for the predictable consequences. Protesters cause
legitimate fears not only in their direct targets, who may deserve it, but
also in their broader audience, as well as in bystanders, fellow protesters, and members of already marginalized groups. Their parents might
say that the inducement of such fear means that their actions invite
additional misunderstandings, and so they must practice additional care.
We might conclude from these points that the use of violence in protest,
even when justified as a defensive and communicative tactic, must meet
additional stringent constraints to mitigate its destructive potential.

The notion that the use of violence requires protesters to exercise more
care in their approach, or take on additional burdens to mitigate the harmful impacts of their communicative techniques, is intuitive but false. We
argue that the use of communicative violence imposes no additional burdens on protesters, though it does, as we argued in chapter 5, place limits
on the moral permission for defense. In part, this mistaken intuition can
be traced to an impoverished view about the conditions that all protesters
must meet. On our view, protesting is an exercise of our political responsibility not simply to speak out publicly against injustice, but to do so in
an effort to try to motivate others to join in the efforts to end it. Given
that obligation, not any kind of communication will do. That protesters
must intend to convey condemnation and motivate others means, at a
minimum, they must consider the context of their communication and the
message they intend to send. In addition, they must analyze the capacities
of their audience as well as attend to the safety and security of bystanders, fellow protesters, and other members of marginalized groups. These
duties are not unique to lawbreaking protesters or violent protesters.

ANALYSIS OF THE COMMUNICATIVE CONTEXT

Returning to Frederick Douglass, we find that an analysis of the communicative conditions at work shapes his understanding of the appropriate response. Douglass did not engage in violent protest, except
insofar as he challenged the authority of the so-called "slave-breaker"
Edward Covey when he was enslaved.[5] Sent to Covey for "reform" by
his master Thomas Auld, Douglass suffered brutally under Covey's
cruelty. He first attempted to reason with his master, Thomas Auld. As

Nicholas Buccola writes, "he appealed to Auld's sense of morality, his professed Christianity, and even the self-interest he had in protecting Douglass as 'his property.'"[6] When Auld refused to help and returned Douglass to Covey, Douglass resolved to respond, which Buccola notes, quoting from Douglass' autobiography, Douglass described as "strictly . . . *defensive*, preventing him from injuring me, rather than trying to injure him."[7] Douglass beat and humiliated Covey. And Covey, according to Douglass, did not attack Douglass again. Buccola argues, "The fight with Covey taught Douglass that when reason and morality fail to bring about change, action may be necessary."[8]

Whereas Buccola contrasts defensive violence with reason and morality, Bernard Boxill argues that they are importantly linked for Douglass.[9] Rather than indicating a loss of faith in the prospects of moral suasion, Boxill contends that such violence is consistent with it, though responsive to a new understanding of the epistemic and motivational barriers to abolition. He notes that the Fugitive Slave Act in 1850 likely motivated Douglass to reconsider violence as a defensive tactic.[10] The Fugitive Slave Act greatly increased the danger for black people, both escaped and free. It made a demand that black people eschew violence, even in defense, that much more of a difficult and unfair burden to bear. It imposed new penalties on other acts of resistance, like assisting escaped slaves, and made the business of slave-catching easier and more attractive. But Douglass' essay, "Is it Right and Wise to Kill a Kidnapper," is striking in that it does not merely defend killing kidnappers on the grounds of justified self-defense. He defends its communicative potential. According to Boxill, Douglass argues that violent self-defense could be morally persuasive to the public who, he thought, tolerated slavery in part on the basis of a false belief that only those who were prepared to defend their freedom with their lives were entitled to it.[11] Defensive violence, he thought, could be a means of persuading the public that enslaved black people had a right to freedom.

Douglass' analysis evolved over time. He continued to analyze the communicative conditions, examine the capacities of his audience, and think through various communicative strategies. By the time he gave his "Speech on John Brown" six years later, his argument for defense had evolved. He moved from an attempt to rouse the conscience of the public by clearing away a false belief that enslaved persons were not fit for freedom, to the view that slaveholders, and perhaps also the public, currently lacked a conscience that could be reached in that way.[12] They had ample evidence, but it had not motivated action. Instead, a more fundamental perceptual shift was necessary. According to Boxill, Douglass concludes that the fear induced by defensive violence could be used to clear the moral vision of slaveholders (and perhaps the public generally).[13]

While Buccola emphasizes rhetoric in Douglass' speeches that seems to place slaveholders outside the realm of moral reasoning, Boxill cautions us to see in Douglass a continued commitment to moral suasion. Though Douglass never claims to have persuaded Covey, rather than having forced Covey to stop whipping him, in Douglass' later understanding of the fight we find reflected the basic elements of a theory of communicative violence, even against those who are currently attacking. He argues, "A man, without force, is without the essential dignity of humanity. Human nature is so constituted, that it cannot honor a helpless man, although it can pity him; and even this it cannot do long, if the signs of power do not arise."[14] By demonstrating his power, Douglass communicated to Covey his dignity and understands his use of purely defensive force as potentially changing Covey's attitude toward him. In addition to pure self-interest, Douglass hypothesizes that this changed social relation between them influenced Covey's decision not to punish him publicly. Douglass provides a roadmap for and a defense of a political philosophy of protest that does not require protesters to always eschew their moral permission for defense.

Dialogic Constraints on Protest

The fact that protest must be publicly communicative gives rise to particular dialogic constraints on it. Kimberley Brownlee, especially, gives a detailed account of these constraints. For Brownlee, the right to lawbreaking protest (and its limits) is grounded in a conscientious moral conviction that is, essentially, communicative. She writes, "This principle of humanism says, first, that society has a duty to honor the fact that we are reasoning and feeling beings capable of forming deep moral commitments, and second, that genuine moral conviction is essentially non-evasive and communicative."[15] The conscientiousness of one's moral conviction, on Brownlee's view, essentially involves "a willingness to communicate our conviction to others."[16]

This dialogic requirement of communication in protest is fleshed out via a number of constraints on its means and modes. As Brownlee says, we must consider whether our chosen means of communication—words, actions, images, body movements, facial expressions—and modes of communication—aggressively, violently, collectively, supportively—are likely to foster understanding in a way that is compatible with the reason-governed, reciprocal, and respectful nature of dialogue.[17]

These dialogic constraints are supported normatively as well as pragmatically. She writes:

> To aim to coerce authorities and society rather than to persuade them would be to treat them as less than fully autonomous beings to whom disobedients could make a reasoned defense of their view. If disobedients are to claim legitimately that they endeavor to engage in moral dialogue, their modes of communication must aim to respect the autonomy of their hearers as rational beings capable of responding to the reasons they believe they have to challenge current policy . . . [In addition,] the constraints imposed by civil disobedients' persuasive aims also have a consequential aspect. Since, as a strategy, coercion and intimidation can turn society against a position, disobedients who sincerely aim to have a long-term impact on policy have reason not to try to force people to adopt their position, but rather rationally to persuade them of the merits of their view.[18]

Thus, she approaches violence cautiously, as a tool that may be appropriate when other means fail. She argues that more radical forms of communication, like violence, require that we first engage in attempts at reasoned dialogue. We disagree—radical forms of communication can be justified when there is a need to encourage a perceptual shift, change social relations, or generate a transformative experience that can remind people of their commitments. Usually, the judgment that this kind of communication is called for will be grounded in failures of more traditional, constrained dialogue to have an effect toward justice. But it doesn't have to be. Evidence that more radical forms of communication are needed could be gleaned in other ways.

When the intention is to communicate toward collective action, the depth and sincerity of that intention—to wit, the extent to which protesters are invested in fulfilling their political responsibility—is measured, in part, by their attention to the communicative context in which they protest. We hold that protesters' modes of communication need to treat both their targets and others as ongoing members of the political community. Morally, this means not attacking anyone except for in defense, refraining from the use of lethal force, and only resolving the tensions between their moral permissions and political responsibility in favor of violence when they have attended to the communicative context.

One might worry that this requirement that protesters attend to the communicative context in which they find themselves before acting in defense places extraordinary demands on them in situations where they may have little time to reflect. Let us be clear: when defense is justified, it is always available to individuals. Our point is that when a person is protesting, they must engage with the communicative context, and seek, as Douglass did, to understand the barriers to bringing about collective action in regard to some injustice, and craft communications that are responsive to the capacities of their audience and those barriers. To refuse to do this is to fail to take up their responsibilities as a protester, though they may still succeed in acting interpersonally, in defense, and politically, as an inspiration or revolutionary.

Prioritizing the Local

The communicative nature of protest is an important reminder of why grassroots, community-based activism and organizing ought to be prioritized over top-down and individual initiatives. All politics are local. Local activism should be prioritized in part because a national campaign to alleviate injustice is unlikely to achieve success without laying significant groundwork. Thus, deference to local politics is a fulfillment of protesters' political responsibility. It is not enough for protesters to say what they believe in a way that reflects their convictions and respects others. Because the responsibility to protest is grounded in the duty to communicate toward collective action, protesters have to actually try to move the needle. This will involve working to persuade others not only of the righteousness of their cause but also to join with them in reshaping the relevant institutions and social structures. Such a charge recommends a bottom-up approach.

While some basic interests are universal, the cultural contours of our practices mean that the nature and shape of an injustice, the reasons people have for perpetuating it, and their epistemic and motivational barriers to collective action, are different across communities. Oppression and privilege manifest and overlap in a multitude of ways, and access to material resources, as well as the kinds of material resources one has access to, all affect the communicative context. Understanding people's interests and uncovering the role that ideology plays in shaping their experiences is the work of sustained critical engagement. This work includes attention to social roles and their effects on epistemic access. For example, in crafting a communication about an injustice, protesters, regardless of their backgrounds, should take care to engage with those who suffer from that injustice. They have intimate knowledge of the oppression they endure and may also have knowledge about past dialogic efforts and their outcomes.

This is a minimal account of the basic features of a communicative process that protesters should follow. But even this might seem to place heavy epistemic duties on protesters and preclude the possibility of spontaneous action or garnering popular support. After all, most protesters—whether lawbreaking or law-abiding—will not have done this work. Recall the criticisms leveled against the 2016 Women's March for its initial failure to engage with the interests of women of color and for crafting a communication that, in the embrace of the "pussy hat" as a symbol of resistance, sidelined the interests and oppression of trans women, in its social meaning if not its intention. Despite these issues, the Women's March was a protest, in that it was a public communicative effort aimed at collective action toward injustice. This dialogic constraint is, in the real world, aspirational, and protesters should aim toward it.

Those who are neither members of the oppressed group, nor otherwise closely connected to the injustice (as members of the local community), can still participate, and participate centrally, in communicative efforts. One lesson Iris Marion Young's model of responsibility is the recognition that all of us are implicated in injustice. There are no outsiders. However, just as individuals stand in different relations to unjust practices in virtue of their social roles—they may be active participants, passive participants, beneficiaries, or victims—so too do they occupy different positions with respect to any protest. They can be the direct targets of a protest action, members of the intended audience, other members of the public, members of the community where the action is taking place, fellow protesters, sympathizers, etc. Attention to these roles can help clarify the content of people's particular political duties in relation to protesting.

The notion of an "outside agitator" is evoked to call all protests—violent and nonviolent—into question. Martin Luther King, Jr. highlights a commitment to grassroots, locally' directed protest while rejecting the evocation of the outside agitator in his "Letter from Birmingham Jail."

In response to questions about why he is in Birmingham he responds that first, he is there because he was invited by community leaders with whom he has organizational ties.[19] Then he writes:

> But more basically, I am in Birmingham because injustice is here . . . Moreover, I am cognizant of the interrelatedness of all communities and states. I cannot sit idly by in Atlanta and not be concerned about what happens in Birmingham. Injustice anywhere is a threat to justice everywhere. We are caught in an inescapable network of mutuality, tied in a single garment of destiny. Whatever affects one directly, affects all indirectly. Never again can we afford to live with the narrow, provincial "outside agitator" idea. Anyone who lives inside the United States can never be considered an outsider anywhere within its bounds.[20]

We might, following Young, extend the bonds of mutuality beyond the bounds of the nation-state that King highlights to the global community with whom we are intertwined through political, economic, and social relationships.[21] Injustice anywhere—in Hong Kong, for example—implicates all and so calls for protest and resistance everywhere.

A Duty to Communicate with Each Other

As a fulfillment of political responsibility rather than an expression of moral conscience, the commitment to engage in the communicative context is one that people owe to each other as members of a political community. In this way, it is similar to the civic virtues defended by Candice Delmas. Delmas argues that people are sometimes required to engage in lawbreaking and uncivil disobedience rather than law-abiding politics to fulfill their duty to resist injustice.[22] Recognizing and fulfilling such obligations requires a level of epistemic awareness and knowledge that typically does not obtain in nonideal contexts replete with ideological infection.[23] Consequently, Delmas argues that all citizens have a duty to cultivate civic virtues of vigilance and open-mindedness. These obligations, particularly the latter, push us toward communication with each other. As Delmas says,

> Through these civic virtues, citizens can form correct beliefs and engage in critical dialog about justice, practices necessary to discharging the obligation to resist injustice. Dialog is essential in no small part because our thinking and motivation are developed with, and political obligations owed to, others.[24]

Delmas invokes an argument from Amélie Rorty that thinking, contrary to how it is usually depicted, is essentially a collaborative activity. We think with others. Similarly, Delmas notes, resistance is usually depicted as an individual activity when in fact, it is most often collaborative.[25] Conscientious objectors and whistleblowers rarely develop their views in isolation or act without others. Usually, people do not protest alone. Most often, when protesters take to the streets it is with others. They depend on a community for collaboration and support. Even lone protesters developed their thinking in community with others (either in-person or virtually) before going public.

It might seem that this demand for dialog and collaboration would preclude the use of violence or more radical forms of protest. We think not. In fact, the commitment to dialog and collaboration does not even preclude the use of violence between fellow protesters or activists. Dialog and collaboration depend on a willing partner. It is a goal and a practice, but it isn't a given.

Young isolated four common excuses that people use to deny that they have a responsibility to rectify structural injustice: reification, the denial of connection, the demands of immediacy, and the claim that it's "not my job."[26] Even those who are engaged, to some extent, in the struggle against injustice can fall into these traps, because they rest on particular ways of seeing the world, which are endemic to political communities. In Young's view, these really do function as excusing or quasi-excusing conditions rather than exercises of culpable bad agency.[27] Transforming these ways of seeing the world is precisely the kind of work that activists must engage in, and such transformations might require communicative violence. As we noted in chapter 5, the demands of immediacy, rather than being a barrier to political action, can instead be appealed to in order to justify violent protest.

The ideological barriers that give rise to these excuses, because they are endemic, exist both among the general public and within activist circles. One way of breaking these barriers within activist groups is the controversial practice of callouts. As Robin Zheng argues, targets of callouts—often members of more privileged groups—report feeling alienated, ashamed, and fearful as a consequence of callouts.[28] They feel that callouts are destructive to movements. Zheng notes that many of these consequences could be from the targets of callouts viewing the practice primarily as one of attributability rather than accountability.

They are assuming that they are liable to a callout on the basis of having done something wrong for which they are responsible, rather than on the basis of being accountable for repairing a harm that they played a role in causing, but that is not attributable to them on the basis of a bad exercise of agency. This is the same mistake that the general public can make in regard to violent protests—sometimes, they are a reminder of political responsibility, not an assignment of blame. Callouts, Zheng argues, can be a means of assigning the forward-looking burdens of repair.[29] She concludes:

> Practices of accountability . . . in the context of rectifying injustice . . . have the logic of reminders—reminders of the fact that because one participates unavoidably in unjust structures, one therefore bears a burden to work toward structural transformation. Reminders, I claim, are critical moral responses because their basic function is to redirect attention, to call upon an agent to stop and reflect on what else she ought to be doing.[30]

Given the tricky nature of political communication, we are not convinced people can always avoid hurting the people with whom they communicate, nor are they responsible for doing so. We can justifiably defend ourselves and others in our interpersonal lives from unjust harm and use those moments politically to call others to account. Recall Douglass' argument that fear can be a powerful tool in clearing the moral myopia of slaveholders. This is not to say that slaveholders bore no liability for their participation in injustice, nor that they were not the justifiable targets of blame. However, that is not the argument that Douglass gives. He argues that fear is justified as a *reminder*. Its function was to force slaveholders to revisit the evidence that they already had and dislodge the epistemic and motivational barriers that prevented slaveholders from attending to their political responsibilities.

In cases where others are shirking their political duties, protesters should engage them in ways that hold them accountable and sustain the possibility of continued interaction. For example, there are things that the person initiating the callout can do to make it more explicitly a practice of accountability rather than attributability, such as directing attention toward the behavior and away from the individual. Similarly, protesters can take care to publicly reaffirm that they are targeting behaviors and, in this way, the system that allows those behaviors to continue.

PROTECTING THE VULNERABLE

The fact that the impact of violence can spill over to a wider audience than is directly targeted is usually both a goal of protest and a tactic that must be wielded with care. One worry is that protesters may inadvertently cause more harm for already marginalized groups through their use of violence.[31] The most disturbing way in which this can occur is through the use of violence as a tactic for dislodging false consciousness in the marginalized.

We have argued that violence is sometimes justified as an accountability practice. While marginalized groups are not culpable for their own marginalization, they are accountable. They perpetuate it through their participation in oppressive practices. Moreover, they are often in the grip of ideologies which explain and justify those practices. Even in cases where the oppressed have little power to affect their circumstances, "waking up" all members of an oppressed group would make it difficult to perpetuate oppression. Also, the marginalized will always have a significant role to play in any social movement, given their epistemic access. Now, it is true that acts of violence are only justified when there is a moral permission for defense. However, one could imagine a protester verbally antagonizing a group of marginalized people in order to gain that moral permission. Worse, perhaps they could claim that their violence was an act of "other-defense" justified on the basis of the unjust harm posed by the oppressed group to themselves. We thereby arrive at a disturbing picture of a "woke" member of a privileged group committing acts of violence against members of a marginalized group in order to produce an ideological transformation that will alert them to the nature of their oppression and remind them of their responsibility toward collective action to "protect them from themselves."

While avoiding flat-footed identity politics, it is clear that this "false savior" is wrong. Their actions reek of the injustices of colonialism and the internment of ethnic minorities in "re-education camps," but the problem with their actions isn't mere condemnation by association. The wrong they commit has less to do with the use of violence against an already marginalized group than with a mistaken application of the dialogic model that protesters must follow. The false savior precludes the opportunity for genuine dialog and collaboration by assuming that they know best, that their actions are necessary to "wake up" oppressed persons who have better epistemic access to their own situation than the "woke" protester. Protecting the vulnerable means, in the first instance, listening to them and working with them, rather than trying to act upon them.

The oppressed may be choosing to subject themselves to particular harms in order to avoid what they (rightly or wrongly) perceive as a greater harm. So, a group of women may choose to subject their daughters to female genital mutilation (FGM) in order to avoid ostracization that would leave their daughters without economic or social resources. Were a group of men to intervene in protest, storming the doctor's office where the women have taken their daughters and using restrained violence to stop the women, hoping to hold them accountable or transform their perspective on the relative harm of these acts, we might rightly criticize the men for their tactics. This critique should not rest merely on their use of violence, but on their refusal to dialog and collaborate with the women.

This doesn't mean that the privileged can never possess important information or be part of an ideological transformation. For example, a right to bodily integrity is universal and the saviors rightly understand that this right is being violated through FGM. But without full engagement with those who are affected by it, they will fail to understand the sociocultural context that undergirds the practice and the concepts which help to maintain and sustain it. This latter issue arises because accountability practices are also about apportioning burdens toward collective action. Those who are marginalized are more likely to bear burdens that are hidden from view or otherwise underappreciated, and so reminding them of their forward-looking accountability for some practices may actually be inappropriate.

As we argued above, the responsibility to publicly communicate toward collective action, when applied to protest, requires protesters to consider carefully their intended audience and analyze their capacities. However, the protesters also need to attend to others, including those who might stand in a special relationship to their protest activities due to their social position and/or other aspects of their social identity. This latter category includes those who live, work, travel through, or own property in the area of the protest, those who identify with (or are identified with) the targets of the protest through familial, social, religious, or political affiliations, and those who suffer from the injustice being protested. Protesters must also be aware of the impact of any protest—violent or nonviolent—on oppressed groups more generally.

In part, the need to attend to such impacts is suggested by the basic political responsibility to communicate toward collective action. Plans to engage in violent protest must take into consideration not only protesters' own interests in defense, but also the interests of those who are party to the violence even though they are not directly targeted by it. If violence is to be a political act, it must be responsive to the political sphere, treating no group as outside of the community. This includes those targeted in protest, as discussed in previous chapters, as well as the intended audience, bystanders, and other members of marginalized groups. Each of these groups has important interests in safety and security that are threatened by the use of violence. This may require protesters to limit certain activities, like property destruction, when its use is likely to alienate large numbers of the political community from a movement. That said, violently protesting via property destruction can send a powerful message to a community in crisis that their pain and anger is felt and shared without indelible damage to future relationships.

One might still wonder whether, given the way that the harms of violence tend to creep outward from the initial target(s) and affect the political community more broadly, its use can ever be justified as part of a social movement. Once the door to violence is open, what prevents others from misunderstanding protesters' use of constrained communicative violence and engaging in much more radical acts that do violate basic rights and dignity? This might be one way to understand Andy Ngo's milkshaking and subsequent beating in Portland.[32] Protesters were carried away by the use of violence and ended up violating his basic rights and dignity. The loosening of an interdiction against throwing things at those with whom we disagree quickly leads to throwing punches and kicking. The concern is that violence, even when constrained and communicative, begets more violence. As Young writes, "There are . . . dangers of disorder among protestors who do go far in righteous rage."[33] Not only will individuals like bystanders become potential victims of circumstance, but also just practices will as well. Furthermore, a breakdown in the rule of law, one might think, threatens the basic rights and dignity of all members of the political community.[34] Even if the state is not legitimate, some rule is preferable to none, particularly with respect to violence. Protecting rights and dignity means upholding the rule of law or, at the very least, supporting those just institutions that do exist.

We reject the suggestion that respecting rights and dignity requires upholding the rule of law. Not only do most people generally accept that respecting rights does not always require compliance with the law (i.e., lawbreaking protest is sometimes justified[35]), but Delmas has also convincingly argued that the same normative principles that ground a duty to obey the law can, even in legitimate states, be marshaled in defense of a duty to disobey the law in order to oppose injustice.[36] Respect for the rule of law is sometimes recommended in the pursuit of securing justice and sometimes not, and it is imperative not to endorse a status quo that trades off the basic rights and dignity of some in order to secure prosperity for others. It is worth taking care to protect just practices where they exist; such practices, and the spaces and contexts in which they emerge, are vital to the success of social movements. But activists are not thereby prevented from moving forward and seeking larger and more drastic social change. In an unjust world, even just practices are inevitably connected to a host of injustices. So, it is important not to be too precious about the small spaces of egalitarianism that may have been carved out.

As a practical claim, the assertion that violence begets violence is not always true. Sometimes, violence can shut down further violence. If this were not the case, defensive war would never be justified. It is possible, and perhaps tempting, to cherry-pick here—those concerned about endless cycles of violence can reference longstanding feuds, while others can reference antifa successes. The pragmatics of violence are complicated and not appropriately summed up by all-or-nothing statements. Furthermore, many contemporary societies are already caught in endless cycles of violence; as Young notes, it is one face of oppression.[37] We are trying to think creatively about how to break out of these cycles, and this involves questioning common assumptions about protest, communication, and violence.

SELF-RESPECT AND VIOLENCE

We have argued that certain communicative contexts recommend the use of violent protest. Our argument focuses on the external benefits of violent protest for communicating toward collective action against injustice and protesters' obligations to seek such benefits. These political obligations are tempered by interpersonal duties to respect others' basic rights and dignity. But one might still wonder about the internal benefits or drawbacks of violent protest. Nonviolence, one might think, is preferable because of the effects of violence on its perpetrator.

That violence sullies not only the message of the protest and its effectiveness but also the protesters themselves is a powerful notion. In a tradition that takes individuals like Gandhi and Martin Luther King, Jr. as its intellectual and practical paradigms, it is unsurprising that their prohibition on violence in the political practice of protest has become deeply entangled with their personal spiritual beliefs and assessments of individual character. Thus, it is worth noting that while both men advocated for nonviolent protest, neither Gandhi nor King were absolutists in their positions on violence. Nor did they see all violence as a reflection of bad character. Gandhi, for example, argues that spontaneous violence is excusable in cases of defense, and preferable to running away, which he views as an expression of cowardice.[38] Cowardice, in Gandhi's view, is itself a form of violence, but one that does nothing to counteract injustice and instead perpetuates it. Better, he thinks, to use violence against injustice rather than add to it.

In a similar vein, King draws a moral equivalence between violence and inaction, writing of the riots in the 1950s and 1960s, "We cannot condone either riots or the equivalent evil of passivity."[39] While King came to eschew violence in his personal life, he does not reject a right to defense. Instead, he is concerned about violence's practical and revolutionary potential.[40] Both men agree that nonviolent resistance requires training—practical and spiritual—and so is not immediately available to all. Such training is necessary in part because the kind of nonviolence that they endorse is far from "peaceable." It inflames tensions and, given the fears and anxieties of oppressors, has the potential to intimidate. In his later writings, King increasingly embraces these elements, advocating for militant nonviolence.[41] Meanwhile, Gandhi moves in the other direction and worries that his campaign has never actually been nonviolent because of its tendency to provoke violence in others.[42]

Not everyone shares these worries about the corrupting influence of violence on protesters' moral characters. In her critique of casting peaceful protest by black Americans during the civil rights era as a case of exemplary democratic sacrifice, Juliet Hooker contends that such a narrative runs roughshod over those black Americans' self-understanding of their protest actions.[43] She argues that black protesters often understood themselves as engaging in acts of defiance, rather than peaceful acquiescence to injustice in the hopes of transforming the hearts and minds of white citizens through their sacrifice.[44] She claims that there is a danger with such defiant, nonviolent acts—they could be read as submission to violence, and so as a humiliation required to get white people to engage in conversations about racial equity.[45] And in fact, some whites and black activists read them as such. In his speech "The Ballot or the Bullet," Malcolm X criticizes marches and sit-ins as not only ineffective at counteracting white supremacy, but also as debasing to those protesters who participated.[46] He argues in favor of black nationalism in part because of its ability to disrupt the attitudes and actions of black Americans away from demonstrations of suffering and vulnerability.[47] Perhaps it is not violence then, but nonviolence that harms the moral character of protesters.

Finally, violence itself may have positive internal effects. Anticolonialist theorist and activist Frantz Fanon argues that it is through revolutionary violence that the colonized subject can both shock the oppressor into recognizing their humanity—a point that echoes Douglass' analysis of the liberatory potential of slave revolt—and transform their own sense of themselves as a self that is worthy of dignity and respect.[48] This second point is also found in Douglass: in his fight with Covey, Douglass' use of violence is not merely a means of enjoining Covey to recognize his humanity and, in light of this, cease his brutal attacks. It also produces a profound internal shift for Douglass, giving rise to a new self-respect. As he writes, "I was a changed being after that fight. I was nothing before; I was a man now. It recalled to life my crushed self-respect, and my self-confidence, and inspired me with a renewed determination to be a free man."[49] The emancipatory effects of violence are not only external but also internal or, as Douglass concludes, "on the spirit."[50]

NOTES

1. Austin Ramzy and Mike Ives, "Hong Kong Protests, One Year Later," *New York Times*, June 9, 2020.

2. Ira Glass, "Umbrellas Down," *This American Life*, July 10, 2020.

3. This echoes Michael Walzer's point about fighting for the kind of world you want to live in that we discuss in chapter 5.

4. Glass, "Umbrellas Down."

5. Nicholas Buccola argues that Douglass' fight with Covey and his reflections on it were influential in shaping Douglass' political philosophy. Nicholas Buccola, *The Political Thought of Frederick Douglass: In Pursuit of American Liberty* (New York: New York University Press, 2012), 89–91.

6. Nicholas Buccola, "Frederick Douglass on the Right and Duty to Resist," Online Library of Liberty, *Libertyfund.org*, May 1, 2017.

7. Buccola, "Frederick Douglass on the Right and Duty to Resist."

8. Buccola, *The Political Thought of Frederick Douglass: In Pursuit of American Liberty*, 91.

9. Bernard R. Boxill, "Fear and Shame as Forms of Moral Suasion in the Thought of Frederick Douglass," *Transactions of the Charles S. Peirce Society* 31, no. 4 (1995), 713–44.

10. Boxill, "Fear and Shame as Forms of Moral Suasion in the Thought of Frederick Douglass," 718.

11. Boxill, "Fear and Shame as Forms of Moral Suasion in the Thought of Frederick Douglass," 719–20.

12. Boxill, "Fear and Shame as Forms of Moral Suasion in the Thought of Frederick Douglass," 720.

13. We discussed this at length in chapter 4.

14. Frederick Douglass, *My Bondage and My Freedom. Part I.—Life as a Slave. Part II.—Life as a Freeman* (New York: Miller, Orton & Mulligan, 1855), 246–47.

15. Kimberley Brownlee, *Conscience and Conviction: The Case for Civil Disobedience* (Oxford: Oxford University Press, 2012), 7.

16. Brownlee, *Conscience and Conviction: The Case for Civil Disobedience*, 29.

17. Brownlee, *Conscience and Conviction: The Case for Civil Disobedience*, 44.

18. Brownlee, *Conscience and Conviction: The Case for Civil Disobedience*, 221, including note 23.

19. Martin Luther King Jr., "A Letter from Birmingham Jail," *The Atlantic Monthly 212.2*, August 1963.

20. King Jr., "A Letter from Birmingham Jail."

21. Iris Marion Young, *Responsibility for Justice* (Oxford: Oxford University Press, 2011), chapter 5.

22. Candice Delmas, *A Duty to Resist: When Disobedience Should Be Uncivil* (New York, NY: Oxford University Press, 2018).

23. Delmas, *A Duty to Resist: When Disobedience should be Uncivil*, chapter 7.

24. Delmas, *A Duty to Resist: When Disobedience should be Uncivil*, 210.

25. Delmas, *A Duty to Resist: When Disobedience should be Uncivil*, 213–19.

26. Young, *Responsibility for Justice*, 154.

27. Robin Zheng, "What Kind of Responsibility do we have for Fighting Injustice? A Moral-Theoretic Perspective on the Social Connections Model," *Critical Horizons* 20, no. 2 (2019), 119.

28. Robin Zheng, "Bias, Structure, and Injustice: A Reply to Haslanger," *Feminist Philosophy Quarterly* 4, no. 1 (2018), 17.

29. Zheng, "Bias, Structure, and Injustice: A Reply to Haslanger," 17.

30. Zheng, "Bias, Structure, and Injustice: A Reply to Haslanger," 12.

31. We introduced this worry in chapter 2.

32. See chapter 3 for our initial discussion of this case.

33. Young, *Responsibility for Justice*, 149.

34. This echoes one of Socrates' arguments in support of obeying the law in the *Crito*. Plato, *Crito*, trans. Benjamin Jowett (Raleigh, NC: Alex Catalogue, 1990).

35. For discussion of this general view, see chapter 1.

36. Delmas, *A Duty to Resist: When Disobedience should be Uncivil*.

37. Iris Marion Young, "Five Faces of Oppression," in *Justice and the Politics of Difference* (New Jersey: Princeton University Press, 1990), 39–65.

38. R. Rajmohan, "Gandhi on Violence," *Peace Research* 28, no. 2 (1996), 34–36.

39. Martin Luther King Jr., "Showdown for Nonviolence," in *A Testament of Hope: The Essential Writings and Speeches of Martin Luther King, Jr.*, ed. James M. Washington (San Francisco: Harper San Francisco, 1968a), 65.

40. Martin Luther King Jr., "Loving Your Enemies," The Martin Luther King, Jr., Research and Education Institute, *kinginstitute.stanford.edu*, November 17, 1957.

41. Karuna Mantena argues that it was King's aim of racial integration as social equality *and* his assessment of the harsh political landscape of racial domination—including its limited prospects for public communication—which led him to endorse nonviolent direct action. He thought it held the best chance of creating change through the dramatic power of public suffering. According to Mantena, this required actively working to dispel the public's fear of black protesters through training and organization, so that they might listen to the protesters' message. Karuna Mantena, "Showdown for Nonviolence: The Theory and Practice of Nonviolent Politics," in *To Shape a New World: The Political Philosophy of Martin Luther King, Jr.*, eds. Brandon Terry and Tommie Shelby (Cambridge, MA: Harvard University Press, 2018), 78–101. It is unclear if King maintained the same theory of communication later in his life, or if he came to endorse nonviolence for other reasons, including the quality of an individual's character. For example, in his final work, *Where Do We Go from Here*, King writes, "I am concerned that

Negroes achieve full status as citizens and as human beings here in the United States. But I am also concerned about our moral uprightness and the health of our souls. Therefore I must oppose any attempt to gain our freedom by the methods of malice, hate and violence that have characterized our oppressors." Martin Luther King Jr., *Where do we Go from Here: Chaos or Community* (Boston: Beacon Press, 1968b), 66. Daniel J. Ott argues that King's endorsement of nonviolence is an aspect of his revolutionary philosophy that sees violence as inextricably linked to existing global economic exploitation and imperialism that reduces people to things. Daniel J. Ott, "Nonviolence and the Nightmare: King and Black Self-Defense," *American Journal of Theology & Philosophy* 39, no. 1 (2018), 70–72.

42. Ronald B. Miller, "Violence, Force and Coercion," in *Violence: Award Winning Essays in the Council for Philosophical Studies Competition*, ed. Jerome A. Shaffer (New York: David McKay, 1971), 37–38.

43. Juliet Hooker, "Black Lives Matter and the Paradoxes of U.S. Black Politics: From Democratic Sacrifice to Democratic Repair," *Political Theory* 44, no. 4 (2016), 448–69.

44. Hooker, "Black Lives Matter and the Paradoxes of U.S. Black Politics: From Democratic Sacrifice to Democratic Repair," 461.

45. Hooker, "Black Lives Matter and the Paradoxes of U.S. Black Politics: From Democratic Sacrifice to Democratic Repair," 461–62.

46. Malcolm X, "The Ballot or the Bullet," in *The Radical Reader*, eds. Timothy Patrick McCarthy and John McMillian (New York: The New Press, 2003), 382–89.

47. Malcolm X, "The Ballot or the Bullet," 382–89.

48. Frantz Fanon, *Black Skin, White Masks*, trans. Richard Philcox (New York: Grove Press, 2008 [1952]), 95; Frantz Fanon, *The Wretched of the Earth*, trans. Richard Philcox (New York: Grove Press, 2004), 51.

49. Frederick Douglass, *The Life and Times of Frederick Douglass*, in *Autobiographies* (New York: Library of America, 1994), 591.

50. Douglass, *The Life and Times of Frederick Douglass*, 591.

BIBLIOGRAPHY

Boxill, Bernard R. "Fear and Shame as Forms of Moral Suasion in the Thought of Frederick Douglass." *Transactions of the Charles S. Peirce Society* 31, no. 4 (1995): 713–744.

Brownlee, Kimberley. *Conscience and Conviction: The Case for Civil Disobedience*. Oxford: Oxford University Press, 2012.

Buccola, Nicholas. "Frederick Douglass on the Right and Duty to Resist." *Online Library of Liberty*. Libertyfund.org. May 1, 2017.

————. *The Political Thought of Frederick Douglass: In Pursuit of American Liberty.* New York: New York University Press, 2012.

Delmas, Candice. *A Duty to Resist: When Disobedience Should Be Uncivil.* New York, NY: Oxford University Press, 2018.

Douglass, Frederick. *The Life and Times of Frederick Douglass.* In *Autobiographies.* New York: Library of America, 1994.

————. *My Bondage and My Freedom. Part I.—Life as a Slave. Part II.—Life as a Freeman.* New York: Miller, Orton & Mulligan, 1855.

Fanon, Frantz. *Black Skin, White Masks.* Translated by Philcox, Richard. New York: Grove Press, 2008 [1952].

————. *The Wretched of the Earth.* Translated by Philcox, Richard. New York: Grove Press, 2004.

Glass, Ira. "Umbrellas Down." *This American Life* (July 10, 2020). https://www.thisamericanlife.org/710/umbrellas-down.

Hooker, Juliet. "Black Lives Matter and the Paradoxes of U.S. Black Politics: From Democratic Sacrifice to Democratic Repair." *Political Theory* 44, no. 4 (2016): 448–469.

King Jr., Martin Luther. "A Letter from Birmingham Jail." *The Atlantic Monthly 212.2* (August 1963).

————. "Loving Your Enemies." *The Martin Luther King, Jr., Research and Education Institute.* Kinginstitute.stanford.edu. November 17, 1957.

————. "Showdown for Nonviolence." In *A Testament of Hope: The Essential Writings and Speeches of Martin Luther King, Jr.*, edited by James M. Washington. San Francisco: Harper San Francisco, 1968a.

————. *Where Do We Go from Here: Chaos or Community.* Boston: Beacon Press, 1968b.

Malcolm X. "The Ballot or the Bullet." In *The Radical Reader*, edited by Timothy Patrick McCarthy and John McMillian, 382–389. New York: The New Press, 2003.

Mantena, Karuna. "Showdown for Nonviolence: The Theory and Practice of Nonviolent Politics." In *To Shape a New World: The Political Philosophy of Martin Luther King, Jr.*, edited by Terry, Brandon and Tommie Shelby, 78–101. Cambridge, MA: Harvard University Press, 2018.

Miller, Ronald B. "Violence, Force and Coercion." In *Violence: Award Winning Essays in the Council for Philosophical Studies Competition*, edited by Shaffer, Jerome A., 9–44. New York: David McKay, 1971.

Ott, Daniel J. "Nonviolence and the Nightmare: King and Black Self-Defense." *American Journal of Theology & Philosophy* 39, no. 1 (2018): 64+.

Plato. *Crito.* Translated by Jowett, Benjamin. Raleigh, NC: Alex Catalogue, 1990.

Rajmohan, R. "Gandhi on Violence." *Peace Research* 28, no. 2 (1996): 27–38.

Ramzy, Austin and Mike Ives. "Hong Kong Protests, One Year Later." *New York Times*, June 9, 2020. https://www.nytimes.com/2020/06/09/world/asia/hong-kong-protests-one-year-later.html.

Young, Iris Marion. "Five Faces of Oppression." In *Justice and the Politics of Difference*, edited by Iris Marion Young, 39–65. New Jersey: Princeton University Press, 1990.

———. *Responsibility for Justice*. Oxford: Oxford University Press, 2011.

Zheng, Robin. "Bias, Structure, and Injustice: A Reply to Haslanger." *Feminist Philosophy Quarterly* 4, no. 1 (2018): 1–30.

———. "What Kind of Responsibility do we have for Fighting Injustice? A Moral-Theoretic Perspective on the Social Connections Model." *Critical Horizons* 20, no. 2 (2019): 109–126.

Chapter 7

Protest and Revolution
Drawing Difficult Lines

The question of violence in relation to politics is difficult in part because, in the liberal tradition, there is no absolute prohibition on political violence. In fact, political violence is positively endorsed in some circumstances, particularly in cases of intolerable political oppression. As Michael Ignatieff writes, "What is the chapter on the dissolution of government in John Locke's *Second Treatise* but a justification of revolution when essential freedoms are usurped? What is the U.S. Declaration of Independence but a reasoned defence of the necessity of political violence to overthrow imperial oppression?"[1] Ordinarily, political violence is prohibited. But when it comes to revolution, it is permitted and perhaps (in some extreme cases) obligatory. Thus, in the liberal tradition, the permissibility of political violence is often used as one of the key distinctions between protest and revolution.

However, this cannot be the correct way to draw a bright line between protest and revolution because, as we have argued, suitably constrained violent protest is sometimes justified, if not required. And importantly, such violent protest is not necessarily revolutionary in nature.[2] In this book, we have argued that clear cases exist of both violent protest (e.g., the protests against police brutality in Baltimore, Maryland, and Ferguson, Missouri in the United States) and nonviolent revolution (e.g., the revolutions in India and Serbia). This is not to say that the Baltimore and Ferguson protests did not contain nonviolent elements, or that the Indian and Serbian revolutions did not contain violent elements; rather, it is to say that the nature of the events overall—that is, whether they

137

count as protests or revolutions—is not determined by their violent or nonviolent characteristics. Violence is not, nor should it be, the marker used to delineate between protest and revolution.

Nevertheless, there is such a distinction, and we articulate it here. First, this is necessary to finish carving out the conceptual space that we contend exists between nonviolent protest and civil disobedience on the one side, and revolution on the other. Second, this is important practically, because whether something is protest or revolution in turn makes distinctive state responses, and interpersonal responses, appropriate. Because revolutionaries are, broadly speaking, enemies of the state, while protesters are not, it makes political sense for the state to treat revolutionaries and revolutions differently than protesters and protests. This is not to say anything about how states *morally* ought to act; that is dependent on whether particular protests and revolutions, and their members, are fighting for justice or not, and the means they are using to do so. The moral question does not obviously rely, then, on determining whether any particular case is one of protest or revolution.[3] But at the political level, a clear distinction between protest and revolution is needed. It matters not only for the state, but also for individuals, who unsurprisingly respond very differently to being asked to protest versus being asked to revolt, and rightly so.

THE TRADITIONAL DISTINCTION
BETWEEN REVOLUTION AND PROTEST

While the permissibility of political violence is usually reserved for revolution in the liberal tradition, this does not yet tell us what revolution is. Classically, revolution is marked out by the desire, and intention, of the revolutionaries to change the political ideals operating in their society, and so severely change, if not dismantle and replace, the governing institutions of their society. Revolution is thus variously described as a "profound and thoroughgoing political transition,"[4] as a "change from an existing form [of government] into some other,"[5] and as the "attempt to change the state fundamentally or to compel a government to step down."[6] While revolution often involves working to change a society's overall form or type of government, it need not. For example, consider the Glorious Revolution of England. Also called the Revolution of 1688, it involved overthrowing James II, the Catholic king, and replacing him with his Protestant daughter Mary and her husband, William of Orange. While England remained a monarchy, this revolution is known as such because it profoundly altered English governance, both in terms of its political ideals and its distribution of power.[7]

By contrast, protest is classically marked out by the desire, and intention, of the protesters to rectify injustices in their society by appeal to their society's existing political ideals. Such appeals are meant to encourage reform or change of institutional rules and structures, without wholesale dismantling and replacing the institutions themselves. We understand protest to include a commitment to a shared political project; while protesters might break particular laws, they nevertheless express a general "acceptance of their [the governing institutions'] authority."[8] This is compatible with rejecting some particular instantiations of governmental authority.

In the 2020 global BLM protests, the popular slogans "Abolish the Police" and "Defund the Police" reject one mechanism of social control by the government (i.e., one governing institution), while appearing to accept the authority of other governing institutions, namely those with the existing political power and authority to abolish or defund the police. Arguably, this is more clearly the case with the slogan "Defund the Police." "Abolish the Police" is ambiguous: it is sometimes a call for existing governing institutions other than the police to do what they currently have the power and authority to do, and it is sometimes a rallying cry for the destruction of all or most current governing institutions. Read in this second tone, "Abolish the Police" is more revolutionary than protestation; read in the first way, it points more toward a fundamental reform than "a rejection of the authority of governing institutions" full stop.[9]

This illustrates one of the complications with drawing a bright line between revolution and protest. There are multiple governing institutions in any contemporary society, and so it is possible to reject the authority of one or some of them without rejecting all of them. People can reject the authority of the police in the United States as a fundamentally corrupt, white supremacist system, and still accept the authority of the U.S. Constitution. The two are connected—they are all part of "the government"—but they are not identical. It is possible to reform, change, destroy, or replace one without doing the same to the other. This is what makes protests possible: protests often work via the mechanism of first drawing out the contradictions between different institutions within a political system, and then calling for reform to bring those institutions into better alignment.

As Martin Luther King, Jr. puts it,

> Throughout Alabama all sorts of devious methods are used to prevent Negroes from becoming registered voters, and there are some counties in which, even though Negroes constitute a majority of the population, not a single Negro is registered. Can any law enacted under such circumstances be considered democratically structured?[10]

King is calling for wholesale reform or change of the electoral system by pointing out the ways in which that institution does not conform to the accepted principles of the U.S. legislative system. He thereby rejects one governing institution by accepting the authority of another as (in principle) just. On the traditional understanding of revolution and protest, this is protest, not revolution.

However, the overhaul of the U.S. electoral system accomplished by the Voting Rights Act of 1965 undoubtedly represents a fundamental political transition. It has been named the most far-reaching and effective piece of legislation ever passed by a U.S. Congress.[11] It changed the United States profoundly by altering both the political power distribution and the instantiation of the political ideal of equality.[12] If we take seriously that a profound and fundamental change to the state is the marker of revolution, perhaps the passage of this Act ought to be viewed as a revolution.

Due to these ambiguities, we interpret the traditional distinction between revolution and protest to be primarily about changes to the political ideals within a society, and secondarily about how those political ideals impact members' acceptance or rejection of the governing institutions of their society. Part of a society's political ideals is a consideration of how political authority is legitimately gained, maintained, and transferred by and among governing institutions. Revolutionaries reject the authority of existing governing institutions because they reject the claim by those institutions that they have attained, maintained, and transferred their political power legitimately. Revolution is thus a rejection of the political ideals that those institutions express and endorse (and usually assert are shared by the society at large). By contrast, protesters accept the political ideals that their governing institutions express and endorse, and that are nominally shared by their society as a whole, and work to hold those institutions to the standards set by those existent political ideals.

Reading the traditional distinction in this way helps to make better sense of historical cases without having to make judgments about the degree of either political or governmental institutional change. The Voting Rights Act of 1965 was the result of protest, rather than revolution, because it worked with the political ideals that were publicly expressed, although not necessarily sincerely endorsed, by the United States' other governing institutions. The Serbian Revolution of 2000 was a revolution, rather than a protest, because it rejected the authoritarian political ideal being expressed and endorsed by Slobodan Milošević and the governing institutions of Serbia, and instead established governing institutions based on a democratic political ideal. This is so even though some theorists have argued that the overthrow of Milošević did not have a profound or fundamental effect on the material or political conditions of many Serbians.[13]

This reading is complicated practically by the fact that revolutionaries can attend a protest, and protesters can occasionally engage in revolutionary action. Members of different camps have been known to help each other out politically, particularly when their political ideals are similar enough to go along with for a time. For example, consider the presence of antifa groups at liberal feminist protests. As Mark Bray suggests, antifa members are often skeptical that liberal feminism goes far enough, but they are willing to lend their support to protests that they view as being a step in the right direction.[14] This points to the complexity of the links between, and divergences among, individuals, events, and movements.

Still, focusing on people's political ideals helps to explain why one is considered a protester while another is considered a revolutionary. The difference is not necessarily their willingness to engage in political activism, but their beliefs about which political ideals their society should have, and their intentions and goals when and if they do engage in activism. For example, whether someone in the United States is a Communist or a Democrat depends partially on what they do, to be sure, but also partially on what they think. If they share the liberal political ideals nominally at play in the United States, they are the latter; if they have a relations-of-production conception of justice, they are the former. Both may be resisting current governing institutions by marching in the streets chanting "Abolish the Police," and if so, they are both resistors.[15] But it is by considering their political ideals that it is possible to categorize them more precisely as protesters or revolutionaries and glean more about their intentions and ultimate goals.

SOME PROBLEMS WITH THE TRADITIONAL ACCOUNT

This traditional distinction between protest and revolution makes sense of a number of historical cases as well as the way in which these descriptors are regularly attributed to individuals. Unfortunately, it has two key issues. First, there is a problem with the notion of shared political ideals. As John Rawls puts it, a society has shared political ideals and, more broadly, a shared conception of justice, when "(1) everyone accepts and knows that the others [in society] accept the same principles of justice, and (2) the basic social institutions generally satisfy and are generally known to satisfy these principles."[16] Rawls admits that societies are rarely well-ordered in this way; this is a description of ideal, or nearly ideal, circumstances. He does contend, however, that generally just societies (i.e., those where revolution is not justified, although civil disobedience may be) have "a certain measure of [public] agreement on what is just and unjust."[17] While there is some disagreement about how to interpret and apply said principles of justice in particular cases, in general, such societies share commitments to avoiding arbitrary distinctions between persons and to creating institutional rules that fairly or properly balance—based on their more-or-less shared principles—competing claims to social advantages.[18]

The difficulty is that even this thinner notion of a shared conception of justice is still too robust to be an accurate description of real-world contemporary liberal societies. Not all members of contemporary liberal societies either fully understand or accept shared political ideals, or interpret them in the same way. This is part of why we have deep political debates. For example, white supremacists accept arbitrary distinctions between persons. They don't think distinctions on the basis of race are arbitrary, but they are wrong about this. And even among those who accept the same basic standards of reason and evidence and express, say, a commitment to equality, their interpretations of equality might vary wildly, such that they are unable to come to a political agreement. While "shared political ideals" is a helpful idea in ideal political theory, it is just that—an idea that primarily applies to ideal political theory. It is not obvious that any actual society has a shared conception of justice even in this relatively thin sense.[19]

To characterize protest, then, it is not sufficient to claim that protest appeals to a society's shared political ideals in order to promote reform or change of existing governing institutions so that they more closely align with those ideals. This assumes a shared conception of justice that does not obviously exist. Moreover, to the extent that societies do espouse some principles of justice and not others, protest often alters these principles either by re-interpreting aspects of them, or by making contested elements of them more salient. The U.S. Civil Rights Movement attempted to reinterpret the ideal of equality, while freedom of speech protests on college campuses ignite debate about the permissions, limits, and relative importance of freedom of speech as contrasted with other ideals, such as safety and inclusion. When protest works, it shifts or broadens a society's shared political ideals (to the extent that the society has shared political ideals at all). It is through these conceptual changes that reform or change is made both possible and more probable.

Similarly, revolutions never actually attempt to completely replace one set of political ideals with another. Rather, revolutionaries work with some considerations of justice that are familiar to their society, while also introducing new, or drawing out less-familiar, elements. The American Revolution is an example. The notion of individual rights was not a new concept, nor one unfamiliar to British and European colonists. American revolutionaries like Thomas Paine merely drew out the implications of individual rights for colonial rule and encouraged their fellow colonists to come to those same conclusions.[20] The same is true of other real-world revolutions: while it might look like a complete overhaul of justice from the outside or to a casual eye, the inner workings of revolutions commonly involve appealing to political ideals already present in their society. The concept of democracy was present in Milošević's Serbia: Otpor! and other revolutionary groups did not bring it in from the outside. Rather, they encouraged its political ascendancy through a variety of methods, including laughtivism (humorous activism), leaflets, strikes, rallies, and volunteering to establish and run polling locations.[21] When revolution works, it does so by appealing to already-present political ideals to introduce the possibility, and probability, of profound political transition and change. It then uses that conceptual impetus to encourage the wholesale restructuring or replacement of existing governing institutions.

Appealing to "shared political ideals" to delineate between protest and revolution does not succeed because on the one hand, it is too idealized and, on the other hand, to the extent that it does exist, it does not reliably track protest and revolution. The second key issue with the traditional distinction is that it delineates between protest and revolution by interrogating the beliefs, intentions, and goals of those involved in the activities in question. However, activists in the streets often do not conceptualize revolution or protest in this way. Some activists certainly do think in terms of political ideals and, more broadly, conceptions of justice, but many others conceive of their beliefs, and subsequent actions, as self-defense, as community defense, as avoiding or mitigating threats, or as a series of last-ditch responses to being pushed to the breaking point.[22] Political activists, like all people, have a wide variety of beliefs, intentions, and goals, which may be in tension with each other, and many of which they may not be able to articulate, even to themselves. To draw the line between protest and revolution based on attributions of particular beliefs, intentions, and goals to those involved in the movements in question, is to risk reducing complex, multifaceted individuals to ciphers and one-dimensional figures.[23]

This problem is not unique. Issues with delineating social and political categories on the basis of belief and intention abound. Criminal law is a salient example: as Nicola Lacey points out, "whilst [intention's] doctrinal and ideological importance is hardly to be questioned, its practical significance at the level of enforcement is very different . . . practical consensus around a clear concept of intention seems as far away as ever."[24] In practice, ascriptions of intention are deeply problematic, in part because we do not have a clear concept of it, and in part because it is, so to speak, in the head, and we don't have access to the inside of people's minds. Some theorists have argued for reading intention off of action, but that is worryingly reductive, especially in light of the ways in which actions carry with them different social meanings depending on the actor's social identity.[25] Our claim is not that beliefs, intentions, and goals do not matter; they surely do. Rather, it is that as a practical matter, we cannot use beliefs, intentions, and goals to draw a bright line between protest and revolution, both because activists have a wide variety of beliefs, intentions, and goals, and because there is no clear-cut consensus on how to appropriately ascribe beliefs and intentions to others.

A political scientist might contend that the traditional distinction is not about shared political ideals, or beliefs, intentions, and goals, but about power: protest is about objecting to, or challenging, certain uses of power, while revolution is about seizing or transferring power itself. Unfortunately, this way of parsing the distinction also does not work. It will describe any democratic system that has built-in contested changes of executive power as an endless series of revolutions. To say that the United States has a revolution every four-to-eight years (when power typically shifts between the two mainstream political parties) seems to stretch the term past all usefulness. In addition, this distinction ignores the fact that one common method of protest is to work to seize power within governing institutions by running and electing so-called protest candidates. The rise of the Tea Party in American electoral politics is a classic case of this: it was without doubt a seizure of power, but to call it a revolution seems inapt, given that the Tea Party is the continuation of a long-running thread of white supremacy in American politics.

We might sharpen this proposed interpretation of the distinction by saying that revolution is the unlawful seizing or transference of power. However, this is too narrow. It cannot make sense of the Glorious Revolution of 1688, the Serbian Revolution of 2000, or any other revolution that used the formal mechanisms of government in order to seize power. Famously, James II and Milošević were both voted out. To fix this, one could deny that these cases count as revolutions proper; however, that begins to look suspiciously like cherry-picking.[26] Moreover, to say that revolution is the unlawful seizing of power depends on having a particular view of what counts as lawful, and that is a difficult question. As Jeremy Waldron notes, lawfulness is an essentially contested concept, because different accounts of law provide different responses to both what is lawful and how lawfulness is determined.[27] Abolishing the police would certainly be revolutionary, and yet it could be done (theoretically) entirely legally. If it were to occur, some would undoubtedly argue—and reasonably so, although not rightly, in our view—that such abolishment is a contravention of the rule of law.[28] While this power-focused reading of the distinction between protest and revolution might be tempting, it does not succeed because it covertly rests on assumptions that are themselves essentially contested and contestable.

A WAY FORWARD

To make headway on this problem, we turn back to our earlier discussions of the essential communicative function of protest.[29] Protest is an attempt to publicly communicate about perceived injustices to two groups: other members of the society generally, and those who have the institutional and systemic power to fix or ameliorate those injustices. More broadly, protest is a way of attempting to create the conditions for public reason in situations and contexts where other kinds of appeals to public reason have not worked, or where the background conditions for public reasoning about certain issues either do not exist or are not widely available. For example, in a society where the existence of institutional racism is not widely acknowledged either by the majority or by those in power, it will do no good to introduce laws, policies, and procedures against institutional racism. Protests can here play a role: by making apparent the presence of institutional racism in a way that is difficult to ignore, it can help to create the necessary conditions for public reasoning about institutional racism. Similarly, in a society where black voices are not heard or taken seriously, their protest signals a plea, or in some cases a demand, to be both heard and reckoned with by their governing institutions. Protest is one of the final modes of *communicative* defense against injustice, to be used when the other public communicative systems of a society—such as its media, legal system, and formal and informal social networks—have failed.[30]

Thinking about protest as communicative defense, for something to be protest rather than revolution it must include the attempted creation of an I-You relationship (to use Stephen Darwall's term) with the opposition.[31] The I-You relationship is second-personal; it involves addressing the other as a "you" who can be given good reasons to act. It thus presupposes that the hearer is an agent open to communication. When the hearer receives or accepts the address or summons, they in turn recognize the speaker as an agent who is communicating with them. This mutual "address of the other as a person" is what Darwall calls "reciprocal recognition," and it is key to providing the right kind of reasons for action.[32]

Reciprocal recognition does not always occur between protesters and those in power, or between protesters and other members of their society. In fact, a lack of second-personal recognition (of the group suffering the injustices in question, by both those in power and other members of the society) is often what leads to the need for protest in the first place. But protest is always partially an attempt to *create* that reciprocal recognition; it treats both the governing institutions and the other members of society as those with whom reasonable communication about injustice is in theory possible. To say it another way, protest tries to talk *to* the governing institutions and other members of society, as well as talking *about* them and the injustices that they perpetuate and maintain.

Protest is communicative in a particular way: it seeks alternately to explain, cajole, plea, transform, and demand, without directly forcing. But because protest often takes place in circumstances the defining feature of which is a lack of recognition of oppressed groups as speakers and hearers (i.e., as "you"s), it first has to create the background conditions for possible mutual recognition by somehow publicly communicating the personhood of oppressed groups. Then, it must communicate the oppression suffered and the redress sought, in ways that at least partially speak *to*, rather than solely *at* or *about*, those in power and those supportive of those in power. In practice, protest can be several different things, and it will have to be. Seeking to broaden the space available for public reason is not easy, especially when the governing institutions and other members of society are not inclined to engage in I-You relationships with members of oppressed groups. Nevertheless, this communicative work is part of what protest essentially seeks to do, in whatever ways are necessary.

By contrast, revolution is not a communicative defense, but rather a deliberately uncommunicative stonewalling of governing institutions. It does not treat those in power, and those supportive of those in power, as persons who could be addressed reasonably, but rather as bodies, or as Darwall writes, as "its" to be managed, controlled, or in the most extreme cases, eliminated.[33] In revolution, there is no mutual recognition between the revolutionaries and the governing institutions of society in the I-You sense that is part and parcel of public reason; rather, there is mutual awareness of each other as objectively powerful forces that can move in, and have an impact on, the world. In revolution, "each watches the other watching him. Neither [the revolutionaries nor the governing institutions of society] relates to the other as a 'you' to whom the first is a 'you' in return. In Martin Buber's terms, the 'I' of each is an 'I-It' rather than an 'I-You.'"[34] This is a fundamentally different stance, at a communicative level, than that of protest. Revolution, unlike protest, does not seek to give good reasons, that is, reasons grounded in the moral relationships characteristic of mutual recognition, for action. At best, it gives first- and third-personal reasons for action. It does communicate about the injustices suffered, and the redress sought, but in such communication, it is not talking *to* the governing institutions of society, but rather *about* those institutions to other members of the society more generally, in hopes that they will be receptive to such third-personal reasons for action.

The American Declaration of Independence is a classic example of this. The Declaration does not seek to establish mutual recognition with King George III and the British government. It is not trying to either begin a conversation or move that conversation forward, into complex public reasoning about justice and injustice. It discusses British rule of the American colonies in a general address to society and provides third-personal reasons (i.e., reasons that are not based on particular I-You moral relationships, but rather on universal moral claims) for why others should disengage, communicatively, with the British governing institutions and come to see them, not as the sorts of institutions that have the potential to be reasoned with, but as forces that must be managed and controlled, if not eliminated altogether.

Like protest, revolution can have, and often does have, many different modes; but one of its essential elements is its use of nonrational influences on the governing institutions of society, in order to overwhelm and (nonrationally) manage, control, or eliminate them. Protest and revolution are not so much about the acceptance or rejection of governing institutions, then, but about communication with those governing institutions. Protest seeks to forge a communicative connection with the governing institutions, and so create the possibility of public mutual recognition and subsequent consensual change, under incredibly difficult communicative circumstances. Revolution seeks to communicate to other members of the society more generally the *impossibility* of such public mutual recognition on the part of the governing institutions, and hence the need for their nonconsensual change.

GRADIENTS, NOT BRIGHT LINES

Once we understand the difference between protest and revolution in terms of their essential communicative features, we gain a better understanding of why it can be difficult to categorize some political actions and movements as protest and others as revolution. Often, protest will come right up to the very edge of being revolutionary; there is a communicative ebb and flow that happens in political protest movements. Some political activism is focused entirely on forging a communicative connection with the governing institutions by working to create the conditions necessary for public reason, and subsequently encouraging public mutual recognition. King's "A Letter from Birmingham Jail" is a classic example of this.[35] As Michele Moody-Adams notes, "what King understood is that moral progress in social and political institutions depends on expanding *perceptual* space—to dislodge prejudices and habits of belief that limit our ability to take a novel view of the world, our place in it, and our relationships to others."[36] By responding to the position of "the white moderate," King opens a public communicative space that did not previously exist—his address transforms his white addressees, both those inside and outside of governing institutions, into people who share his view of justice. This crafting of white Americans' perception of justice makes public reason about segregation, and institutional racism more broadly, possible. Subsequently, King is able to engage in mutual recognition with the "white moderate" that he has created to encourage them to support institutional justice–oriented change.[37]

Ideally, such "discursive reason-giving and argument" would be sufficient to persuade the governing institutions and other members of the society to change course.[38] However, this form of protest, which takes up a model of liberal academic explanatory communication, is "often ineffective at bridging the barriers that divide us."[39] Sometimes, actions that are further along the spectrum toward revolution are necessary. Such actions still carry with them an essentially communicative aspect; but rather than engaging in discursive reason-giving and explanatory argumentation, they attempt to alter the perceptual space of their society's governing institutions, and its other members, via other modes of communication.

Consider Richard Spencer (a well-known American neo-Nazi) getting punched in the face while giving an interview on live TV.[40] Such an action is not explanatorily communicative in the way that "A Letter From Birmingham Jail" is; nevertheless, it is not wholly uncommunicative either. As Thomas Nagel writes, "in our culture it is an insult to punch someone in the mouth, and not just an injury."[41] This is why such a punch "seem[s] appropriate . . . [it is directed] to that which makes him an object of . . . opposition."[42] In this case, Spencer's support of fascism is what makes him a target. Punching him in the mouth on live TV conveys not only the puncher's disagreement with Spencer's position, but also communicates that some views are so abhorrent and insulting that they should not be voiced, much less endorsed.[43]

Due to the insulting nature of a punch to the mouth, such an action actually takes up the I-You relationship, both toward Spencer and—because of the public nature of the punch—toward the governing institutions and other members of the society. It recognizes Spencer (and others who might share or disavow his fascist positions) as a "you" who can be not only injured (and thus managed or controlled) but also insulted (and thus as an agent who can be reasoned with, in theory).[44] Because of its social and political meaning, some nonlethal violence can be publicly communicative in the right—that is, protest-oriented—kind of way. This is not to say that it is therefore justified; moral and pragmatic considerations also play a role, as we have argued throughout, in determining whether any particular instance of nonlethal violence is justified. But it is to say that such nonlethal violent political activism, when at least part of its communicative nature is an attempt to engage in public mutual recognition or to create the perceptual space necessary for public mutual recognition, is protest rather than revolution.

As we noted earlier, political movements contain a multiplicity of particular actions, each of which approaches revolution to a greater or lesser degree. To put it bluntly, there is a gradient between liberal academic explanatory communication and the guillotine. The guillotine is undoubtedly revolutionary, because it is impossible to engage in mutual recognition with those who are dead. This is why lethal violence cannot be protest. To be sure, the guillotine is communicative to other members of the society, but its use is not a way of engaging in public reason, or creating the conditions for engaging in public reason, with the governing institutions of the society. But before the guillotine, there are a plethora of political actions (some violent, some not) which approach, but do not reach, that extreme. Trying to determine in advance which particular kinds of political activism count as protest and which as revolution is likely to fail. Instead, it is better to interrogate the communicative aspects and functions of different political actions as they occur, bearing in mind that attempts to jar, broaden, or transform governing institutions' and other members of the society's perceptual spaces, and so engage in public mutual recognition with them, can—and often will need to—take many and varied forms.

This way of distinguishing between protest and revolution not only makes sense of paradigm historical cases, but also enables the tentative categorization of political actions and movements as they occur in the contemporary world. Although it is essential—given both the fractured nature of political movements and the ideological infections to which people are subject—to be careful and thoughtful with such categorizations, it is also important that people be able to make them, at least provisionally, in real time.[45] By focusing on the communicative elements in play, people can begin to determine appropriate and inappropriate state and interpersonal responses to political activism without having to rely on their often knee-jerk responses to violence and insult. For example, graffiti is, legally speaking, property destruction, and to the powerful represents a serious breakdown of social order. But certain kinds of political graffiti, such as Banksy's refugee piece and his mural of Steve Jobs in Calais, explicitly attempt to create the conditions necessary for public reasoning to occur between the governing institutions of society and its oppressed members.[46] Despite their revolutionary overtones, such graffities are protestations and should be treated as such.

Opening the conceptual space between nonviolent protest and civil disobedience, on the one hand, and revolution, on the other, carves out room for more kinds of political activism to count as protest without abandoning the tenets of liberalism. Liberal societies, rather than dismiss nonlethal political violence out of hand as revolutionary, should first listen. They should consider whether such violence is an attempt to forge a communicative connection based on public mutual recognition (under incredibly difficult communicative circumstances) with their governing institutions and other members of their society. If it is, then such violence is protest, however close it may be to revolution.

NOTES

1. Michael Ignatieff, *The Lesser Evil: Political Ethics in an Age of Terror* (Toronto: Penguin Canada, 2004), 91–92.
2. For this argument, see chapter 2.

3. One exception here may be Kant, who famously argues that revolution is never justified. Immanuel Kant, *Perpetual Peace, and Other Essays on Politics, History, and Morals* (Indianapolis, IN: Hackett Publishing Company, 1983).

4. Matthew Noah Smith, "Rethinking Sovereignty, Rethinking Revolution," *Philosophy & Public Affairs* 36, no. 4 (2008), 408.

5. Aristotle, *Politics*, trans. Benjamin Jowett (New York: Digireads.com, 2017), 5.I.

6. Christopher J. Finlay, *Terrorism and the Right to Resist: A Theory of Just Revolutionary War* (New York: Cambridge University Press, 2017), 21.

7. Steven C. A. Pincus, *1688: The First Modern Revolution* (New Haven: Yale University Press, 2009).

8. Smith, "Rethinking Sovereignty, Rethinking Revolution," 408.

9. Smith, "Rethinking Sovereignty, Rethinking Revolution," 408.

10. Martin Luther King Jr., "A Letter from Birmingham Jail," *The Atlantic Monthly 212.2*, August 1963.

11. Chandler Davidson and Bernard Grofman, "Editors' Introduction," in *Quiet Revolution in the South: The Impact of the Voting Rights Act, 1965–1990*, eds. Chandler Davidson and Bernard Grofman (New Jersey: Princeton University Press, 1994), 3–17.

12. Ryan M. Crowley, "'The Goddamndest, Toughest Voting Rights Bill': Critical Race Theory and the Voting Rights Act of 1965," *Race Ethnicity and Education* 16, no. 5 (2013), 696–724.

13. Marija Zurnić, *Corruption and Democratic Transition in Eastern Europe: The Role of Political Scandals in Post-Milošević Serbia* (New York: Palgrave Macmillan, 2019); Nenad Dimitrijevic, "Serbia After the Criminal Past: What Went Wrong and what should be Done," *International Journal of Transitional Justice* 2, no. 1 (2008), 5–22.

14. Mark Bray, *Antifa: The Anti-Fascist Handbook* (Brooklyn, NY: Melville House, 2017), esp. chapter 6.

15. For a discussion of the relationship between resistance and protest, see chapter 1.

16. John Rawls, *A Theory of Justice, Revised Edition* (Cambridge, MA: Belknap Press, 1999), 4.

17. Rawls, *A Theory of Justice, Revised Edition*, 6.

18. Rawls, *A Theory of Justice, Revised Edition*, 5.

19. Of course, we can appeal to the written political documents of a society, such as its Constitution, for guidance about the political ideals formally espoused in that society. However, just because certain political ideals are formally espoused, does not mean either that they are widely accepted, understood, or communally interpreted, or that the governing institutions of the society either do or seek to satisfy them.

20. Thomas Paine, "Common Sense," in *The Writings of Thomas Paine*, ed. Moncure Daniel Conway (New York: G.P. Putnam's Sons, 1894).

21. *Bringing Down a Dictator,* Documentary, directed by Steve York (New York: PBS, 2002).

22. Chad Kautzer, "Notes for a Critical Theory of Community Self-Defense," in *Setting Sights: Histories and Reflections on Community Armed Self-Defense*, ed. Scott Crow (Oakland, CA: PM Press, 2017), 35–48.

23. Not to mention the risk of treating disparate political activities and activism as all being part of some monolithic movement. For more on this worry, see chapter 2.

24. Nicola Lacey, "A Clear Concept of Intention: Elusive Or Illusory?" *The Modern Law Review* 56, no. 5 (1993), 621.

25. For more on social meanings, see especially chapters 3, 4, and 6.

26. One might say that some cases of revolution are peripheral, while others are central, and so we can arrive at the core concept of revolution by focusing on the central rather than the peripheral cases. However, as Joseph Raz points out, it is not clear that there is any non-circular way of determining which cases count as central and which as peripheral. Joseph Raz, "Two Views of the Nature of the Theory of Law: A Partial Comparison," *Legal Theory* 4, no. 3 (1998), 257.

27. Jeremy Waldron, "Is the Rule of Law an Essentially Contested Concept (in Florida)?" *Law and Philosophy* 21, no. 2 (2002), 155–57.

28. While Waldon does not speak specifically to the question of abolishing the police, his discussion is relevant here. Waldron, "Is the Rule of Law an Essentially Contested Concept (in Florida)?", 137–64.

29. This discussion begins in chapter 1 and continues throughout the book.

30. Rawls, *A Theory of Justice, Revised Edition*, 327–28.

31. Stephen Darwall, *The Second-Person Standpoint: Morality, Respect, and Accountability* (Cambridge, MA: Harvard University Press, 2006), chapter 1. We use "opposition" here broadly, to refer not only to those who actively oppose the protests and their goals, but also to those who do not support the protests and their goals.

32. Darwall, *The Second-Person Standpoint: Morality, Respect, and Accountability*, 39–40.

33. Darwall, *The Second-Person Standpoint: Morality, Respect, and Accountability*, 40.

34. Darwall, *The Second-Person Standpoint: Morality, Respect, and Accountability*, 40.

35. King Jr., "A Letter from Birmingham Jail."

36. Michele Moody-Adams, "The Path of Conscientious Citizenship," in *To Shape a New World: Essays on the Political Philosophy of Martin Luther King,*

Jr, eds. Brandon M. Terry and Tommie Shelby (Cambridge, MA: Harvard University Press, 2018), 282. Emphasis in original.

37. Our interpretation of King's project here owes much to Tommie Shelby and Brandon M. Terry's discussion of King's political philosophy. Tommie Shelby and Brandon M. Terry, "Martin Luther King, Jr., and Political Philosophy," in *To Shape a New World: Essays on the Political Philosophy of Martin Luther King, Jr*, eds. Tommie Shelby and Brandon M. Terry (Cambridge, MA: Harvard University Press, 2018), 1–16.

38. Moody-Adams, "The Path of Conscientious Citizenship," 282.

39. Moody-Adams, "The Path of Conscientious Citizenship," 282.

40. Justin Wm Moyer, "Richard Spencer, White Nationalist Spokesman, was Punched in the Face on Camera in D.C." *Washington Post*, January 20, 2017.

41. Thomas Nagel, "War and Massacre," *Philosophy & Public Affairs* 1, no. 2 (1972), 135, note 7.

42. Nagel, "War and Massacre," 135.

43. Bray, *Antifa: The Anti-Fascist Handbook*, introduction.

44. To insult someone, you must first see them as a person—an agent—with the capacity for reason and thus insult. David Livingstone Smith, "Paradoxes of Dehumanization," *Social Theory and Practice* 42, no. 2 (2016), 416–43.

45. To give a quick example of the practical importance of such categorizations, consider that use of military force is often considered an appropriate state response to revolution, but not to protest. Some states use "security forces" to respond to both protest and revolution, which is problematic for a whole slew of reasons, not least of which is that it does not encourage careful distinctions by those in power between concerned citizens and enemies of the state.

46. Suzanne Moore, "Banksy's Refugee Piece shows Us how to Protest – and Grieve," *The Guardian*, January 25, 2016.

BIBLIOGRAPHY

Aristotle. *Politics*. Translated by Jowett, Benjamin. New York: Digireads.com, 2017.

Bray, Mark. *Antifa: The Anti-Fascist Handbook*. Brooklyn, NY: Melville House, 2017.

Crowley, Ryan M. "'The Goddamndest, Toughest Voting Rights Bill': Critical Race Theory and the Voting Rights Act of 1965." *Race Ethnicity and Education* 16, no. 5 (2013): 696–724.

Darwall, Stephen. *The Second-Person Standpoint: Morality, Respect, and Accountability*. Cambridge, MA: Harvard University Press, 2006.

Davidson, Chandler and Bernard Grofman. "Editors' Introduction." In *Quiet Revolution in the South: The Impact of the Voting Rights Act, 1965–1990*, edited by Davidson, Chandler and Bernard Grofman, 3–17. New Jersey: Princeton University Press, 1994.

Dimitrijevic, Nenad. "Serbia After the Criminal Past: What Went Wrong and what should be Done." *International Journal of Transitional Justice* 2, no. 1 (2008): 5–22.

Finlay, Christopher J. *Terrorism and the Right to Resist: A Theory of Just Revolutionary War*. New York: Cambridge University Press, 2017.

Ignatieff, Michael. *The Lesser Evil: Political Ethics in an Age of Terror*. Toronto: Penguin Canada, 2004.

Kant, Immanuel. *Perpetual Peace, and Other Essays on Politics, History, and Morals*. Indianapolis, IN: Hackett Publishing Company, 1983.

Kautzer, Chad. "Notes for a Critical Theory of Community Self-Defense." In *Setting Sights: Histories and Reflections on Community Armed Self-Defense*, edited by Crow, Scott, 35–48. Oakland, CA: PM Press, 2017.

King Jr., Martin Luther. "A Letter from Birmingham Jail." *The Atlantic Monthly 212.2* (August 1963).

Lacey, Nicola. "A Clear Concept of Intention: Elusive Or Illusory?" *The Modern Law Review* 56, no. 5 (1993): 621–642.

Moody-Adams, Michele. "The Path of Conscientious Citizenship." In *To Shape a New World: Essays on the Political Philosophy of Martin Luther King, Jr*, edited by Brandon M. Terry and Tommie Shelby, 269–289. Cambridge, MA: Harvard University Press, 2018.

Moore, Suzanne. "Banksy's Refugee Piece shows Us how to Protest – and Grieve." *The Guardian,* January 25, 2016. https://www.theguardian.com /commentisfree/2016/jan/25/banksy-refugee-protest-political-street-art-stik -stewy.

Moyer, Justin Wm. "Richard Spencer, White Nationalist Spokesman, was Punched in the Face on Camera in D.C." *Washington Post,* January 20, 2017. https://www.washingtonpost.com/news/local/wp/2017/01/20/richard-spence r-white-nationalist-spokesman-was-punched-in-the-face-on-camera-in-d-c/.

Nagel, Thomas. "War and Massacre." *Philosophy & Public Affairs* 1, no. 2 (1972): 123–144.

Paine, Thomas. "Common Sense." In *The Writings of Thomas Paine*, edited by Moncure Daniel Conway. New York: G.P. Putnam's Sons, 1894.

Pincus, Steven C. A. *1688: The First Modern Revolution*. New Haven: Yale University Press, 2009.

Rawls, John. *A Theory of Justice, Revised Edition*. Cambridge, MA: Belknap Press, 1999.

Raz, Joseph. "Two Views of the Nature of the Theory of Law: A Partial Comparison." *Legal Theory* 4, no. 3 (1998): 249–282.

Shelby, Tommie and Brandon M. Terry. "Martin Luther King, Jr., and Political Philosophy." In *To Shape a New World: Essays on the Political Philosophy of Martin Luther King, Jr*, edited by Tommie Shelby and Brandon M. Terry, 1–16. Cambridge, MA: Harvard University Press, 2018.

Smith, David Livingstone. "Paradoxes of Dehumanization." *Social Theory and Practice* 42, no. 2 (2016): 416–443.

Smith, Matthew Noah. "Rethinking Sovereignty, Rethinking Revolution." *Philosophy & Public Affairs* 36, no. 4 (2008): 405–440.

Waldron, Jeremy. "Is the Rule of Law an Essentially Contested Concept (in Florida)?" *Law and Philosophy* 21, no. 2 (2002): 137–164.

Bringing Down a Dictator. Documentary. Directed by York, Steve. New York: PBS, 2002.

Zurnić, Marija. *Corruption and Democratic Transition in Eastern Europe: The Role of Political Scandals in Post-Milošević Serbia*. New York: Palgrave Macmillan, 2019.

Index

About the Authors

Jennifer Kling is assistant professor of philosophy and director of the Center for Legal Studies at the University of Colorado, Colorado Springs. Her research focuses on moral and political philosophy, particularly issues in war and peace, self- and other-defense, international relations, protest, and feminism. She is the author of *War Refugees: Risk, Justice, and Moral Responsibility* (2019), as well as numerous articles in academic journals and edited collections.

Megan Mitchell is associate professor of philosophy at Stonehill College in North Easton, Massachusetts, where she teaches classes in philosophy of race, feminism, and African philosophy. Her work is in political philosophy, particularly issues of race and racism. She has authored articles in *Dialogue: Canadian Philosophical Review, Ethical Theory and Moral Practice, Radical Philosophy Review,* and *Pacifism, Politics, and Feminism: Intersections and Innovations* (2019).